LEARNING
TO FLY

America's Cup XXXIII 2010

LEARNING TO FLY

By Roger Vaughan

Photographs by Gilles Martin-Raget

Choptank Word Bank

The Roger Vaughan Library

Learning to Fly
America's Cup XXXIII 2010

Published by Choptank Word Bank
Bachelor's Point, Oxford, Maryland
www.choptankwordbank.com

ISBN: 978-1-7333135-2-0
Library of Congress Control Number: 2020922394

Cover and Interior Design: Joseph Daniel
www.storyartsmedia.com

POD Edition
Printed in the United States

For Kippy

PROGRESSION

"If it's tension you're looking for, we have tension."

Larry Ellison
Skipper and Owner,
BMW Oracle Racing

The America's Cup has always been a focused quest to find a design breakthrough, a quest that takes place behind locked doors. Usually, progress is sluggish, and there are often blind alleys that slow momentum. Vaughan has a special talent for talking with people about their motives, skills, mistakes and triumphs. His writing style is fluid. Each page is filled with fascinating details about how this unusual America's Cup campaign evolved. We watch, amused, as a group of talented monohull sailors is introduced to the idiosyncrasies of multihulls. We marvel at how designers and builders wrestle with confounding issues. We learn why both Ellison and Coutts made the difficult decision not to steer the boat. And that the first time the boat sailed around a full-length Cup course, without breaking something, was the first race of America's Cup XXXIII.

The team worked with unusual selflessness behind the unifying goal of winning the America's Cup. Larry Ellison has a reputation for being somewhat of a recluse, but we watch him, and Russell Coutts, setting goals and motivating people to achieve success under the most difficult circumstances. At critical junctures, Ellison is on hand to make the big decisions.

Learning to Fly is an illuminating read for any sailor. There are many lessons here that apply to all endeavors in life.

Gary Jobson
Annapolis, Maryland

his team to design, build, and sail the most advanced multihull ever conceived. It was an effort that could easily have foundered many times along the way. For everyone involved it was an emotional roller coaster ride, complicated by different levels of the State of New York courts vacillating in its rulings for and against both teams.

Ellison and his team CEO, three-time America's Cup winning skipper and Olympic Gold medalist (Finn) Russell Coutts, demonstrated remarkable grit that never wavered throughout the unnerving setbacks that almost doomed their effort to create a super multihull powered by an enormous wingsail. As you read this story of steadfast leadership under stressful conditions, you'll frequently wonder, "What would I have done?" Ellison and Coutts recruited an international cast of skilled team members, all of whom brought innovative ideas to the table. The boat was built in the State of Washington. Training took place in San Diego. The America's Cup was eventually raced off Valencia, Spain, in light winds during the winter month of February. Just moving the boat and all its pieces was a logistical nightmare any military commander would appreciate.

Every day the boat went sailing, some critical piece of equipment would break. In any race, you must finish to win. The team had to find ways to realize the boat's immense potential while keeping it in one piece. A lifelong racing sailor who can ask probing questions, Vaughan quotes all the key players about how they tackled problems.

Few challengers have won on their first try. Larry Ellison, like many sailors before him, came up short in his first two challenges. He persisted with a third attempt that started off with a dispute over the Defender's plan to name a brand new yacht club as the Challenger of Record. The legal, technological, and human saga that raged over the next two and half years went well beyond any Hollywood script.

The failure of Defender and Challenger to agree on a yacht to be used in the 2010 competition resulted in a race held in yachts whose basic specifications are firmly set forth in the Deed of Gift, the original document that governs the event. Thanks to San Diego's success in having a multihull accepted for its defense in 1988, those 2010 yachts became multihulls. It would be the first time in history that two multihulls squared off in an America's Cup match. Learning to Fly provides a critical, missing piece of Cup history, bridging the gap between 159 years of monohulls sailing for the Cup, and the boats that are now foiling for the Cup.

Roger Vaughan takes us inside Ellison's BMW Oracle Racing campaign, representing the Golden Gate Yacht Club on San Francisco Bay. Vaughan tells us in illuminating detail how Ellison and his team of managers, designers, builders and sailors created an extraordinary yacht to take on Ernesto Bertarelli's *Alinghi*, representing Switzerland's Societe Nautique de Geneve. The media referred to the challenge as "a battle of the billionaires," but that description was too simple. Learning to Fly is a fascinating narrative about how Ellison's relentless determination inspired

Introduction
THE MISSING PIECE

The 169-year quest to win the America's Cup has provided us with a remarkable legacy of how highly-motivated, passionate sailors put everything they have into the pursuit of winning the Auld Mug. The America's Cup game attracts individuals who are used to winning at everything they do. But in this ultimate arena – the world's oceans -- success has many facets, and is most elusive. That's what makes competing for the Cup, or watching the competition, so intriguing. Since 1851, challenging for the oldest sporting trophy in the world has often become an impossible dream for the world's most powerful, otherwise successful people. Ask Thomas Lipton, who failed five times. Defending teams have won 29 out of the 35 America's Cup regattas that have been held over this long stretch of time.

FEBRUARY 12, 2010

It's a cold winter morning, still dark outside at 6:30 a.m. in Oxford, on Maryland's Eastern Shore, in the United States. I am bundled in fleece, bent over my computer as I have been the last two mornings in hopes of seeing Race One of America's Cup XXXIII, an event that has been delayed a couple years by a protracted legal battle. I have ESPN360 loaded on my laptop. ESPN's sailing analyst Gary Jobson and his color man, two-time Tornado Olympic silver medalist Randy Smyth, are in a little studio in Bristol, Connecticut, commenting on the live video feed from Valencia, Spain, spontaneously, as they see it, at the same time I see it. It's cold in Valencia, too, with tem-

---

Protest on the first encounter. Race 1 pre-start, USA 17 *enters the starting area on starboard tack with speed, and nails* Alinghi.

peratures in the high 40s. Weather has caused a further two-day delay. This morning there's a four-hour delay waiting for wind, but finally there is a countdown on the screen over pictures of the two fastest big sailboats ever designed and built. Their crews line the boats up for the entry into the box, or starting area, which according to the rules must be made after the five-minute gun. I find myself leaning forward on my seat at the sight of these extraordinary boats — the Swiss defender, *Alinghi*, a catamaran; BMW Oracle Racing's *USA 17*, a trimaran — because they are so huge, so frail-looking with their enormous masts carrying so much sail area perched on comparatively small frameworks of floats and crossbeams, the whole lash-up held together with wire cables. In the aerial shots, they look like giant water striders. The crewmen look tiny. During a water-level shot of *USA 17* flying a hull, I notice the angle of heel increases perceptibly. As a former Hobie 18 sailor, I flinch (watch out!), because there is a sense that the edge is near, and precipitous. Unlike with my Hobie, if one of these exotic, space-age machines goes over, there is no tomorrow. The 108- and 115-foot (LOA) multihulls appear as the sailing equivalent of Formula 1 cars, flirting with the wall on every corner. Yes, Mr. Ellison, there is plenty of tension to be felt, even 4,000 miles away on my small screen.

Then the boats are entering the box, *USA 17* from the right, with starboard advantage (determined by a draw), *Alinghi* from the left. *USA 17* has a head of steam. It must be moving at 20 knots plus, its wave-piercing floats slicing through the water like hot knives through butter. *Alinghi* is not moving quite as fast, and the wide shot makes it obvious that unless the Swiss crew does something *right now*, there is no way their boat will get out of *USA*'s way. Perhaps underestimating the closing speed of 35 knots or more, *Alinghi* elects to come head to wind, maybe tack, but that's always a slow process in a multihull, which has no momentum to speak of when de-powered, and suddenly it is a dead duck. *USA* has to alter course to avoid *Alinghi*. *USA 17*'s protest flag goes up. The on-the-water umpires quickly raise *Alinghi*'s colors. It's a port/starboard violation, a no-brainer. Incredible. After almost a four-year wait, the first race of America's Cup XXXIII begins with a penalty to *Alinghi* incurred on the first-ever encounter between the two boats, less than a minute into the pre-start.

KIWI MAGIC

The story of America's Cup XXXIII begins in 1993 in Woodside, California, with an exchange of emails between Larry Ellison and his neighbor, yachtsman David Thomson. Ellison is the co-founder and CEO of Oracle Corporation, a software and hardware company that at the time is the largest privately held company in the United States. Ellison wrote to Thomson: "Want to do the Transpac and win?" Thomson replied, "Is the Pope a Catholic?"

Larry Ellison, Co-founder, Chairman of the Board, and Chief Technology Officer of Oracle Corporation; skipper and owner, BMW Oracle Racing in 2010.

Thomson's and Ellison's children were attending the same school. The two fathers had gotten to know one another watching their kids play soccer. When Ellison found out Thomson enjoyed yacht racing, he sent him the email. When a brief conversation left no doubt that Ellison was serious, Thomson contacted a fellow sailor named Bill Erkelens, who was running boats during summer vacations from college, and supervising club-level racing programs with his girl-friend (eventually his wife), Melinda. "I had a lot of respect for Bill and Melinda," Thomson says. "They were wonderful college kids with ability and integrity. Bill had sailed a lot with me in the 1980s and '90s."

Thomson and the Erkelenses began looking for a good Transpac 70 they could charter that could win. But the maxi rule was in flux, and they ended up hav-ing Bruce Farr design a new 80-footer that Cookson (NZL) would build. Ellison, who has a lifelong inter-est in Japanese culture, named the boat *Sayonara*.

"Our first race out was Oakland to Catalina," Thomson says, "a feeder race to get the boats south for the 95 Transpac. We creamed the record on Larry's first offshore race. We had Paul Cayard on board, Geoff Stagg from Farr, Stan Honey, Joey Allen, Robbie Naismith, a great crew of guys. Then we got second across the line in the Transpac, did the Big Boat Series in San Francisco, and that was another disappointment. We got 2nd. There was gnashing of teeth and pulling of hair."

Sayonara would become famous for taking line honors in the storm-savaged Sydney to Hobart Race of 1998, in which six sailors perished. That was the first in a notable run of victories for the boat that included the Kenwood Cup, three Maxi World Championships, two Chicago–Mackinac races, Antigua Sailing Week, and the St. Francis Big Boat Championship, to name a few.

"I remember during that first race to Catalina," David Thomson says, "Paul Cayard was trying to raise funds for his America's Cup campaign. He asked Larry if he'd be interested. Larry was adamant that he would never, ever do an America's Cup." Ellison doesn't remember that conversation, but he was adamant that he didn't want to be the person who broke up Team New Zealand. "There were a lot of TNZ guys on *Sayonara*," Ellison says. "I didn't want to race against them. I thought of them as my team."

Ellison's mind changed at the awards dinner at the end of Antigua Sailing Week in 2000. Tony Rae, a particularly gregarious New Zealander, one of several members of the TNZ America's Cup squad who had been sailing regularly with Ellison on *Sayonara*, had a chat with Ellison that evening about challenging for the Cup. "Trae" did it in the insistent, casually friendly, always understated, but personally challenging way that New Zealanders have turned into an art form. Call it Kiwi magic. They know just when to break the tension with a big old laugh that says "just kidding" (not). Mark "Tugboat" Turner, another Kiwi who is co-head of Core builders, which built BMW Oracle Racing's 90-foot multihull and its 247-foot wingsail, had joined the *Sayonara* program in 1995, six months before that boat was launched. Turner was at the Antigua awards dinner.

"Tony started on Larry," Turner says, "said come on, you need to do the Cup. We'll all be there to help. You have to remember that we had Brad Butterworth, Robbie Naismith, Joe Allen, Steve Wilson, Tony Rae, and myself on the boat, a pretty good contingent of Team New Zealanders. And the OneWorld Challenge had just burst its bubble and was on the market. It was a discussion that went on all night with Tony and Larry." [One World Challenge, an America's Cup syndicate out of Seattle, Washington, had made financial overtures to TNZ as early as 2000.]

Rae, who has been with Team New Zealand since its inception in 1987, remembers. *Sayonara* had won Antigua Week. When the awards were delayed for some reason, Rae figured Ellison might get impatient and leave before they called his name for the silverware. That had happened before. Seeing Ellison at a table by himself, he went over to talk with him.

"I walked over and crouched down beside him," Rae says, "and we talked about the regatta, then got into other races he had planned for the boat. He had some questions, and I might have mentioned how we organized things at TNZ. I may have mentioned the America's Cup. Larry said tell me more about the Cup, so I did, told him what it involved. He said he'd like to do the Cup, he could do it. I was taken aback. I said it was a little different than a maxi campaign. He asked what he'd need to do it. So I talked him through how TNZ was set up.

"He said he had a design team, the Farr office. I suggested they might be committed to someone else, and he said no, we can get them. I figured maybe he could. I'd been talking about sponsors, and he said we don't need sponsors, we can do it now. I enjoyed the conversation. It's amazing to talk with someone like Larry about the Cup, someone who can make decisions about it. Most people are wondering how to get sponsors, how to raise enough money to put an entry in, or get a design team. He just jumped a few fences and was ready to push the button.

"I had a bit of a sweat on. I thought, hang on, wait a minute. And he said we've got a sailing team, a good starting point, Bill and Melinda can start hiring people. We'd been talking half an hour. It was amazing how long the prize-giving was delayed. I was crouched down so long I had cramps in both legs. I looked around and saw Bill Erkelens looking daggers at me as if to say, what the hell are you talking to Larry about? And Larry says, get Bill over here, I want to tell him we're going to do an America's Cup program, where is he?

"Bill went a bit white when I told him why Larry wanted to see him," Rae says. "Afterwards he said he couldn't believe I talked Larry into doing this. He was thinking they'd build a new maxi and he'd have some time off back home in Newport."

Ellison chuckles when he remembers that evening in Antigua. "Trae certainly was an instigator," he says. "Brad too. But poor Tony should take most of the blame. In the end he stayed with TNZ. He encouraged me to do the Cup, then said no, I'm not going to sail with you. The guys who made the decision to leave went with Russell. The guys who had been sailing with me elected to stay with TNZ. We ended up without many TNZ guys, and that hurt our team."

Ellison says he likes sailing with Kiwis because they represent a broader cross section of the population than American sailors. "A lot of US sailors are kids from wealthy families," Ellison says. "If you are a US sailor, chances are your parents are well off, belong to a yacht club, and you sailed in the youth program. In New Zealand, if your father is a cop or a plumber and you are a seven-year-old girl, you'll be out there in a P-class boat learning to sail. I didn't come from a privileged background. I feel more comfortable sailing with Kiwis."

Bill Erkelens also remembers that evening in Antigua. He says someone grabbed him and said he'd better get over to Ellison's table because there was serious discussion going on. Ellison left Antigua the next morning. Erkelens and Turner delivered the maxi to Newport, Rhode Island, for a regatta that summer. The day he arrived in Newport, Erkelens got a call from Ellison, asking if he had signed anyone up yet. "I said no," Erkelens says. "I told Larry I figured if it were really serious he'd call me and we'd talk more about it. And he said no, let's go."

By then, Ernesto Bertarelli, head of the Alinghi Swiss team, had made his offer to Russell Coutts, Brad Butterworth, and four other key crewmen from TNZ. "I thought if Team New Zealand is really breaking up, maybe I will do the Cup," Ellison says.

Melinda Erkelens, who was mate on *Sayonara* (she handled the pit with Bill during races), recalls buying a bunch of file folders in various colors and setting up shop on a table in the Erkelenses' Newport apartment. "Larry was hot to trot," she says. "We figured we'd better get some America's Cup boats. That was the first emergency. We got the boats acquired from Paul Cayard's America One team. They were in New Zealand. And we bought the Aloha syndicate's boats in Hawaii." Melinda Erkelens also has a law degree. In 2000, she became general counsel for Oracle Racing, the America's Cup syndicate.

People were a parallel priority. Tom Ehman, a sailor with four North American championships to his credit, and whose America's Cup rules and administrative involvement began in 1980, was one of the first calls. Ehman was living in Hamburg at the time, working for Formula 1. Bill Erkelens recalls they had a shot at getting Brad Butterworth. "We had an offer from Brad," Bill says. "The money seemed ridiculous. Now it seems like a bargain. We would have won the Cup with those guys. There would have been no Alinghi. But at the time it seemed like too much money."

LEARNING CURVE

After a while, one gets used to hearing BMW Oracle Racing team members referring to anything but a win as a disaster. That attitude surely emanates from the team's boss, Larry Ellison, who is known as a ferocious competitor. Several books have been written about Ellison, one of the premier businessmen of his era. Ellison was, for a time, in 2000, ranked as the world's wealthiest individual. (One book, by Karen Southwick, is titled *Everyone Else Must Fail*.) While on paper, the 2003 Oracle Racing (as it was then named) campaign did quite well for a first effort. It made the Louis Vuitton challenger finals, losing to *Alinghi* five races to one. With Russell Coutts skippering and Brad Butterworth calling tactics, *Alinghi* went on to trounce Team New Zealand 5–0 in America's Cup XXXI, giving Coutts a remarkable 14–0 record in America's Cup matches.

Making the 2003 Louis Vuitton finals against nine teams from six countries that raced 120 races over a five-month period was no small accomplishment for a freshman syndicate. And Oracle's defeat by Alinghi in the Louis Vuitton finals was much closer than the score (5–1) indicates. Several races could have gone either way. But the Oracle program was characterized by a raft of skippers coming and going, an endless game of musical chairs that was played out in the back of the boat. But the real problem, according to insiders, was the relative slowness of the boat. "It really didn't matter who was driving," Bill Erkelens says. "The Farr office gave us a grid of 100 boats to choose from. We went for a narrow, high-stability boat with a small sail area, and it turned out to be not such a good choice. Alinghi selected a more conservative, more full-bodied boat, and won the day."

Ellison weighed in on some major decisions during the Oracle campaign, but staffers say he wasn't involved on a regular basis with the team. Ellison commented afterward that running an America's Cup syndicate was more like running Oracle (the corporation) than *Sayonara*. Welcome to the America's Cup learning curve.

Ellison went quiet for a few weeks after being eliminated in the challenger finals of America's Cup XXXI. Staffers began packing up the gear without a clear idea if Oracle would continue on as a challenger. Several key players began checking plane schedules. Melinda Erkelens says she had a feeling, and cautioned a few of them not to leave town. Sure enough, a few days later Ellison called her. He'd received a draft of a Protocol for America's Cup XXXII from Alinghi attorney Hamish Ross. Ellison was enthusiastic. Melinda called Tom Ehman, head of external affairs. "I said ask him to send it for us to look at, and don't sign anything!" Ehman says. "We'd had previous conversations with the Alinghi guys about ways to modernize the Cup. But this was a rush job of getting some of that stuff on paper before they had even won the Cup. It was a pretty one-sided document."

Ehman, Melinda, and Ian "Fresh" Burns, from the design/performance team who has been involved in America's Cup since 1984 (with the exception of the 1988 rogue challenge that pitted a catamaran against a monohull), sat down in Auckland to negotiate the AC XXXII Protocol with Alinghi. The Swiss boat was leading Team New Zealand 3–0 in the final match, with the outcome predictable given the rash of breakage that had been suffered by TNZ. "We even had a couple sessions on Bertarelli's yacht, *Baba*, during a race," Ehman says.

Ellison had laid the groundwork with Bertarelli. In the course of several meetings on their motor yachts during the challenge round, the two men had become friends. "Bertarelli had asked Larry to be Challenger of Record," Ehman says. "Larry had decided to do it before Alinghi had won the Cup."

Oracle Racing — now BMW Oracle Racing, with the German auto maker increasing its commitment — not only continued its quest for the Cup, but became the Challenger of Record (COR) for America's Cup XXXII, to be held in Valencia, Spain, in 2007. Being COR did not guarantee a good outcome. No COR has ever made it to the challenger finals, let alone won the Cup. It was also the first time in Cup history that the regatta would be held outside the country that had won it. But the Deed of Gift (originally signed in 1857) that governs this regatta strongly suggests that the match be sailed on ocean courses free of headlands. That left Switzerland out as a venue.

Part of the Cup modernization plan was a so-called "home and home" series between BMW Oracle Racing and Alinghi to promote America's Cup Class racing between Cups. First was the Möet Cup, held on San Francisco Bay in September, 2003. The second round was the UBS Trophy, to be held in Newport, Rhode Island, the summer of 2004. BMW Oracle Racing won both events, professional, and owner/driver series.

By all accounts, AC XXXII was a success. It was

the first America's Cup to be held in Europe since the initial race around the Isle of Wight in 1851 that started what is described in the Deed of Gift as a "friendly competition between foreign countries." (One can almost hear the authors of the Deed snickering as they wrote that line.) As a result, high excitement was bubbling from the outset. The society pages were touting Valencia as the place to be seen during the racing season. The huge marina-type "campus" housing all the team headquarters and the surrounding facilities, which had been constructed in Valencia, was architecturally striking. The sheer magnitude of the 20-acre project was most impressive.

The final Protocol called for a series of "Acts," match and fleet racing regattas to be held among the 12 challenging teams in four locales: Spain (Valencia); France (Marseilles); Sweden (Malmo); and Italy (Trapani) during 2004, 2005, 2006, and early 2007. The idea was to build interest throughout the continent, and the world, in a new, revived America's Cup with European flavor. The logistics were daunting, but in the end the racing was good, and well-attended. The Acts were well-publicized, and accomplished their task.

BMW Oracle Racing broke COR tradition by making it to the semifinals of the Louis Vuitton Cup, there to be defeated by Italy's *Luna Rossa*, four races to one. *Luna Rossa*'s co-helmsman was a 27-year-old from Australia named James Spithill (remember that name). Italy was in turn defeated in the Louis Vuitton final by Emirates Team New Zealand, setting the stage for the most closely contested Cup match in memory.

The battle between ETNZ and *Alinghi* was full of drama right down to the hair-raising finish of Race 7, with ETNZ nearly pulling off a win despite having to complete a 360-degree penalty turn before the finish in extremely light wind. *Alinghi* beat them across the line by one second, winning the match five races to two.

Participants felt proud to have been part of such a successful, compelling event. The greater America's Cup community praised the Swiss and their Challenger of Record for putting on such a good show. The television audience was large. Expectations for the future of the Cup were high. A modern standard had definitely been established.

THE PROTOCOL – JULY 5, 2007

The rosy afterglow of America's Cup XXXII lasted exactly two days. Alinghi won the America's Cup on July 3, 2007. On July 5, 2007, Alinghi released its Protocol for the next America's Cup. The only elements in the Protocol that weren't met with hue and cry were the date set for the next match (July, 2009), and the venue selected (Valencia). Chief among the problems with the Protocol was the selection of the COR, whose critical responsibilities include negotiating, with the defender, a level playing field for the regatta. Alinghi had selected Club Náutico Español de Vela (CNEV), which no one had ever heard of. Many, including BMW Oracle Racing, felt the brand-new (as it turned out) club did not satisfy the conditions set down in the Deed of Gift. In fact, CNEV had no members, no premises, no phone number. It was an instrument of Alinghi. And that was the tip of the iceberg.

Other contestable points of the Protocol:

• ACM would set the rules for racing, and could sanction or restrict competitors as it saw fit.

• Alinghi would gain the advantage of entering the challenger series as it pleased, therefore gaining the ability to effect the result or even exclude a competitor at no risk to itself.

Larry Ellison read the Protocol and was appalled. Russell Coutts, who had been in conversation with Ellison about joining BMW Oracle Racing as CEO, was equally dismayed. With two Cup campaigns behind him, Ellison now knew what was involved. With Coutts virtually signed up, he had the leadership he wanted. On July 9, 2007, Ellison decided to file a "legitimate" challenge through the Golden Gate Yacht Club in San Francisco, which had been acting as Oracle Racing's official challenging yacht club since America's Cup XXXI in 2003.

Melinda Erkelens rang up Tom Ehman and design coordinator Ian Burns after she'd heard from Ellison that he wanted to file a challenge. They convened in Burns's Valencia apartment and worked for two days around the clock to produce a set of legal papers for a legitimate challenge. They flew to Geneva on July 11 to deliver their brief to the secretary general of Société Nautique de Genève (SNG), the defending Swiss yacht club represented by Alinghi. The cover letter read (in part) as follows:

We respectfully submit that the challenge [from CNEV] is invalid. Among other deficiencies, it is not from a bona fide yacht club, but from an entity organized in the form of a yacht club only a few days before the challenge was accepted by SNG, and which has never had an annual regatta on an open water course on the sea or an arm of the sea as required by the Deed of Gift. It is also apparent that this "Challenger of Record" has not performed the duties of the Challenger as contemplated by the Deed of Gift, but has simply delegated to the Defender the authority to determine all of the "conditions" governing the match. This undermines the fundamental purpose of the Deed of Gift to preserve this competition as a Challenge Cup.

Attached is a bone fide challenge from the Golden Gate Yacht Club (GGYC). GGYC hereby demands recognition as the legitimate Challenger of Record for the 33rd America's Cup...

"I had spoken with Bertarelli on the phone," Larry Ellison says, "and I said let's go back to the rules of the 32nd America's Cup and we'll get on with it. I don't understand these new rules where the umpires work for you. I said, Ernesto, why are you doing this? And he said, Larry, wouldn't you do this if you had won the Cup? Wouldn't you like a set of rules like this? My answer was no, I really don't think I would feel good about winning if I couldn't lose.

"Ernesto is a peculiar guy with a peculiar perspective on the world, and regarding who wins and loses. I beat him in the owner/driver Möet Cup in San Francisco back in 2003, and I won the first two races of the UBS Cup in Newport. In the third race we broke our spinnaker pole, which he went on to win. During dinner on his boat that evening he said, Larry, I'm not enjoying this, I don't want to sail against you anymore. I said fine, we can stop. And he said okay, but I win this regatta. The first two races were worth one point, and the third race was worth two points, so we are tied, but since I won the last race, I win the regatta. I said, Ernesto, you're kidding, right? And he said no, I'm not kidding. I said okay, I'll see you on the starting line tomorrow. And I won the last two races. But it was surreal. And this is when we were friends.

"I think everyone was happy with the way America's Cup XXXII went off, then here Ernesto came with this crazy set of rules. It's very hard to respect anyone who would set up rules for a competition so only he could win."

Legal Update – July 20, 2007

GGYC files suit in New York Supreme Court against SNG asking the court to void the challenge of CNEV; declare the Protocol governing America's Cup XXXIII null and void; declare GGYC's challenge valid; and require SNG to participate in establishing a proper Protocol, or proceed with a match against GGYC under rules set forth in the Deed of Gift.

RC

An Olympic gold medalist in the tough, single-handed Finn Class (Los Angeles, 1984), Russell Coutts (*below*) won his first America's Cup when he skippered Team New Zealand to a 5–0 sweep of the

USA's *Stars & Stripes* in 1995. It was New Zealand's fourth try for the Cup. After a five-year delay, Coutts and Team New Zealand defended the Cup in 2000, in Auckland, sweeping the Italian team 5–0. In a gracious gesture, Coutts gave the helm to his understudy, Dean Barker, for the last race.

BY ROGER VAUGHAN • PAGE 35

Not long after that victory, the Cup world was stunned by the brash raid on the New Zealand team conducted by Swiss pharmaceuticals magnate Ernesto Bertarelli, who, in a flash, introduced free agency to the America's Cup. Bertarelli hired not only Coutts, but his tactician, Brad Butterworth, main trimmer Warwick Fleury, headsail trimmer Simon Daubney, strategist Murray Jones, and Dean Phipps, who handled runners and other back-of-the-boat jobs. This crew had suddenly become the core of the Swiss Alinghi team, said to be named after a "word" uttered by Bertarelli's small child.

Bertarelli's move paid off. In 2003, Alinghi won the Louis Vuitton Cup, and swept Team New Zealand in the final of America's Cup XXXI, 5–0. Coutts had won three Cups as skipper without losing a race, a record he shares with the legendary Charlie Barr, who had compiled his record in the America's Cups of 1899, 1901, and 1903, and Dennis Conner, who won in 1980, 1987, and 1988. [Conner won a 4th Cup as starting helmsman and tactician on *Courageous* in 1974.]

But Coutts would have a falling out with Bertarelli over contract disputes. On July 26, 2004, Alinghi issued a press release announcing Coutts's termination from the team. Coutts, to his credit, kept a low profile, refusing to take his case public. It's difficult to say who was more disappointed about Coutts's absence from America's Cup XXXII: Coutts, or Cup watchers who were eager to see if he could add to his spotless record. But Coutts's contract dispute kept him from sailing for Alinghi, or joining another team until XXXII was in the record books. Not long after Race 7 on July 3, 2007, Coutts and Ellison began conversations.

"I honestly don't remember if I called Larry, or he called me," Coutts says. "But I thought he was the one who could afford to do a Cup campaign properly. We started talking right after the Cup in 2007. I was amazed at how quickly he made the decision and we got on with it." Coutts pauses. "I think I may have called him, initially." BMW Oracle Racing announced Russell Coutts as the team's new CEO on July 24, 2007.

Larry Ellison recalls that he definitely called Coutts. "But Russell said he was expecting the call," Ellison says. "That means if I had not called him, he was planning to call me. Going after Russell was an easy decision. He had clearly managed the Alinghi team brilliantly, and without the largest budget. He raced us in the final, where he steered beautifully, but more important was how he had prepared the team for the Louis Vuitton Cup, and the America's Cup. He had a boat well-suited for match racing. It was capable of being tuned to different modes to suit for different situations."

Coutts says he liked a lot of what he saw when he arrived at BMW Oracle Racing. "We kept the good things, and moved on from there," he says. "Frankly, I'm experienced at the America's Cup game, which may or may not mean I'm a good manager elsewhere, but the initial key appointments were very important. And we didn't get too many wrong in this campaign. Mike Drummond, our design director, was a key. Stephen Barclay, our COO, was a key, and James Spithill, 31, our helmsman, is a fantastic talent. I don't necessarily think I did as good a job managing the whole thing from start to finish as I did in 2003. But we made the big decisions better than the opposition did, and that was the really big key."

As Cup campaigns go, 2003 was a bit more straightforward. Coutts ran a two-boat monohull program, and trained his team for a traditional match race. At first, America's Cup XXXIII looked like more of the same. But all too soon, that would change into what Coutts ended up calling "The Logistics Cup."

Legal Update – November 27, 2007

"The court concludes that CNEV's challenge is invalid, and that GGYC is Challenger of Record pursuant to the Deed."

BMW Oracle Racing's first big win in court came after several months of motions, cross-motions, and direct communications, including a letter from seven challengers opposing the Alinghi Protocol, a letter from Coutts to Alinghi offering to work out a compromise, and a six-page settlement offer signed by Coutts and general counsel Melinda Erkelens.

Efforts to mediate continued after the court declared GGYC the Challenger of Record. On December 4, 2007, Coutts wrote to his old tactician and golfing buddy Brad Butterworth, with whom he had won three America's Cups, re-stating the amendments BMW Oracle Racing had written to the 33rd Protocol and Competition Regulations, and concluding:

Time is running out, and a key requirement for all competitors is certainty. If there are any points in this proposal that are unacceptable to you we would ask that you negotiate these with us as soon as possible. We are approaching a point where we have to know what sort of race we will be competing in. It is simply not feasible to carry on trying to be prepared for both a conventional regatta and a Deed of Gift race. Accordingly, we request that you indicate if you accept the proposals set out above as soon as possible.

Coutts did not receive a reply. But the headline in the December 11, 2007, *Tribune de Genève* said it all: "Alinghi will defend in a multihull."

Coutts was amazed. "We'd won the court case, we'd sent what I thought was a good settlement offer to Alinghi, our second one, and I thought for sure it would settle it. Then the Swiss newspaper came out. I was driving into the base the next morning, thinking about it. As it happened, we were having a monohull design meeting that morning, reviewing tank test data from two models. John Reichel and others were sitting around the table. So we had a bit of a discussion, then I said, hold on, stop the meeting. Bertarelli has announced a multihull program. The longer we keep hoping for a settlement, the less time we're going to have. We've got to get ready. We've got ten months. Each day we don't address this is a day wasted. From today on we shift focus to a multihull.

"There was a stunned silence around the table," Coutts recalls. "But Reichel and the others agreed. Imag-

Russell Coutts, team CEO, addresses a design meeting.

ine the sailing team. None of us had sailed multihulls very much. There were lots of glum faces. It wasn't looking like what we had signed up for. There was a major shift in focus, not to mention terrible time constraints."

90 X 90 X 3 X 20

From the time GGYC challenged the validity of CNEV, the possibility of foregoing the usual challenger trials and having a match race between BMW Oracle Racing and Alinghi had always been in the wings. This is known as a "Deed of Gift" (DOG) match. The Deed accounts for that eventuality in a paragraph beginning, "In case the parties can not agree on the terms of a match . . ." If that clause kicks in, it follows that "the parties" have not settled on a boat, or even a formula for a boat to be used in the competition. A 90-foot monohull had been initially suggested by Alinghi in the Protocol, but once Alinghi lost in court on the validity of CNEV, it declined to negotiate any terms with GGYC. Therefore the boats had to conform to another clause in the Deed specifying that absent agreement otherwise, competing vessels, "if of one mast, shall not be less than forty-four feet nor more than ninety feet on the load water-line." In the case of a DOG match, both teams will obviously go for the maximum LWL allowed. The Deed also contains this line: "if [the competing yachts or vessels are] of more than one mast they shall not be less than eighty feet nor more than one hundred fifteen feet on the load water-line." Why neither BMW Oracle Racing nor Alinghi opted for a second mast and an additional 25 feet of waterline is a bit of a mystery.

The vision of 90-foot LWL monohulls is intriguing, harking back to the golden, olden days of the Cup when the typical yacht's overall length was 130 feet or more. But in 1988, New Zealand's Michael Fay got severely tripped up when he pursued that line of thinking with his "rogue challenge" of the San Diego Yacht Club, and its representative, Stars & Stripes. What tripped up Fay was San Diego's response with a multihull half the length of Fay's 90-foot LWL monohull sloop. The multihull was deemed valid after a pitched, precedent-setting, seesaw battle in court resulting in a mismatch that was a yacht-racing travesty. The 1988 match – and the 1870 match, in which Franklin Osgood's *Magic* bested James Lloyd Ashbury's *Cambria* (UK) -- were only other ones where the challenger and defender could not agree on a class of boat and other details, so the donor's "default rules" contained in the Deed of Gift prevailed. When it comes to a DOG match, since they were legitimized in 1988, multihulls will always be the boats of choice simply because for a given length they are so much faster.

When Larry Ellison decided to file a challenge at midnight, on July 9, 2007, three things had to happen. Melinda Erkelens rushed off to get a new agreement signed with Golden Gate Yacht Club. GGYC had been Ellison's official challenger through two Cups, but his formal agreement with them had expired. Tom Ehman got the challenge paperwork together with a little help from the aforementioned Michael Fay. "He and Andrew Johns [Fay's attorney, and his rules expert in 1988] were most supportive throughout," Ehman says. In fact Faye and Johns visited the team base in Valencia and provided Ehman with their challenge papers from 1988. Ehman says he virtually copied them. Third, Ian Burns was charged with coming up with the dimensions of the challenging vessel, a Deed of Gift requirement.

Burns immediately called Michel Kermarec, a multihull expert living in France, and a member of the BMW Oracle Racing team. Kermarec, who is often referred to as a "genius" within the BMW Oracle Racing ranks, took less than a morning to

From left: Design Director Mike Drummond, Russell Coutts, and multihull expert Michel Kermarec at work.

get back to Burns. "I was having dinner with friends when Fresh called," Kermarec says. "He asked me what was the fastest 90-footer we could build. Having worked and sailed on several of the ORMA 60-foot multihulls in France, I knew these very fast boats had evolved to being nearly as wide as their length. So the answer to Fresh's question was evident to me: a trimaran with the maximum length permitted by the Deed of Gift, and as wide; 90 feet by 90 feet." Other dimensions Kermarec suggested: 3-foot draft with daggerboards up; 20-foot draft with daggerboards down. Even on paper it looked like an awesome beast.

"In the technology of velocity-prediction programs," Ian Burns says, "Michel is the best I've ever seen. He was convinced from the outset a trimaran would be superior to a catamaran. He based that on his experience designing big, all-purpose, round-the-world multihulls. It was a big decision because whatever we submitted was what we had to show up with on the starting line. It was huge. And to his credit, Michel stood by his decision. He never wavered. During the campaign some of our guys would look over the fence and think Alinghi, with their catamaran, had it figured out, and they'd wish we had a cat. But Michel always said we would be faster, equal or better across the range of conditions."

At that point in the program, no one really believed the multihull would become a reality. The dimensions were submitted as a placeholder. BMW Oracle Racing always thought that after the court ruled on CNEV's legitimacy, BMW Oracle Racing would be able to agree to a conventional, multi-challenger event with Alinghi. That proved impossible. Then came the *Tribune de Genève* headline.

DOG RACE

"The worst thing that happened with this whole thing is the sailors really got screwed by Alinghi"
— Larry Ellison.

The button had been pressed, the green lights were flashing, the alarm claxons were going off, but there was a brief moment before the full-out, two-year scramble of design, building, and sailing began — and before the legal battles continued — when every part of BMW Oracle Racing paused to deplore the implications of a DOG race. There were at least ten other teams, roughly a thousand people, not counting subcontractors, that had been made redundant with a single Swiss newspaper headline. Ten America's Cup teams would be either shut down or reduced to skeleton staffs while they waited for Alinghi and BMW Oracle Racing to conclude their business. It was not a good moment for the subculture that revolves around the America's Cup. AC XXXII had seemed to get the contest for the oldest trophy in sports back on track after the interminable, weather-delayed, and one-sided set of races in Auckland that was AC XXXI. Momentum for fans and sponsors was building. And now, this.

"There was an aura of disbelief in the shop when we were told the 90-foot tri was a reality," said Tim Smyth, the co-head of BMW Oracle Racing's Core Builders in Anacortes, Washington, north of

Mark Allen "Tugboat" Turner (top) and Tim Smyth (bottom right), co-heads of Core Builders. Smyth discusses a construction detail (bottom) with chief boat builder, Michel Marie.

Seattle. Smyth started life with degrees in economics and politics. Before he knew it, he was sailing with a yachtsman he'd met in London who decided to build a new boat in Spain. Smyth, who had built a couple canoes with his father, pitched in, enjoyed it, and was good at it. "It was a typical New Zealand story," Smyth says. "Go forth, travel overseas, and see what happens to you." Quite a bit happened to Smyth. With his Spanish connections and a twist of fate, Smyth ended up building Spain's America's Cup yachts for the 1989–90 campaign. He followed that with a one-tonner for Juan Carlos, the king of Spain, before building several Whitbread, then Volvo 60s. In 2001, Smyth moved to Washington State, and began building boats for Larry Ellison.

"We all believed in our hearts it was going to be a 90-foot monohull," Smyth says. "We knew it would be exciting to do a trimaran, but bloody hell, it would be huge. There were other ramifications. The elimination of the other teams would leave a bad taste in our mouths. It wasn't something we wanted to happen. We were reluctant planners, if you like."

BMW ORACLE RACING 90

But the turn had been called, and BMW Oracle Racing came out of the blocks like a class-A dragster, with wheels smoking. Unlike a dragster, the trimaran had a bit more than a quarter mile ahead of it. With the basic decision to build a trimaran having been made, BMW Oracle Racing turned to the design firm

Design Director Mike Drummond.

of VPLP (naval architects Marc Van Peteghem and Vincent Lauriot Prévost) in France. VPLP has broad experience with multihulls, having done everything from 30-to-60-foot racing multis to the eye-popping

138-foot luxury cruising multihull *Douce France*. On the competitive side, VPLP is best known for the Groupama boats, a series of 60-foot ocean tris successfully campaigned by Frenchman Franck Cammas. With time of the essence, and the only design parameters being to come up with a boat for an unknown venue with unknown wind conditions and an unknown sea state, the team decided on a scaled-up version of the Groupama concept.

Design director Mike Drummond had been convinced the trimaran was faster in concept. Drummond had been with TNZ as structural designer and backup navigator in the successful 1995 campaign. He also got involved on the performance side, working with VPP on appendage design. In 2000, when TNZ successfully defended the Cup, Drummond got more involved with the overall design of the yacht, and came up with the concept for a new rig configuration that became standard until America's Cup XXXII in 2007. On board, he split the navigation chores with New Zealand's celebrated Tom Schnackenberg. Drummond moved to Alinghi in 2007, where he worked with the design team in the role of "customer," keeping tabs on the big picture. He was also involved in the development (with North Sails) of 3Di sailcloth. Again, he was navigator on the boat. He moved to BMW Oracle Racing when he got a call from Russell Coutts offering him the job of design director.

"It sounded like a more interesting role," Drummond says. "I would have been repeating myself if I'd stayed with Alinghi. At BMW Oracle Racing I was free to put a design team together. It was a step forward." (After his fourth win, Drummond was inducted into the America's Cup Hall of Fame, in 2010.) But Drummond was a stranger to trimarans. "I'd been sailing an 18-foot A-Class catamaran for three or four years," Drummond says, "but never a tri."

Among those at Drummond's first design meeting were two Frenchmen with a world of experience in multihull design and construction. They were Michel Kermarec, who had produced the 90 by 90 dimensions for the Challenger of Record submission, and Hervé Devaux, a structural engineer who had designed the composite structures for many of the big French multihulls. Devaux also did the structural design for the wing mast on *Stars & Stripes*, the catamaran that won the Cup in 1988. "Devaux has good practical knowledge not just of structures," Drummond says, "but of how yachts behave and the loads they encounter. Kermarec's proficiency with VPP studies and focus on appendages were invaluable. Both guys provided huge strength for the team. Based on their experience in the ORMA 60 class," Drummond says, "both Devaux and Kermarec thought the tri would be faster. The ORMA 60 class is open to catamarans, but the tris are faster. Having a center hull means you can carry forestay and mainsheet loads more efficiently. A main hull with the volume aft means you can shape the main hull for slower speeds. Putting the volume forward in the floats works better for high speed. Experience says trimarans also maneuver better, and have better sea-keeping ability in waves."

Drummond figures the Alinghi side went for a catamaran because that was where their experience lay. Ernesto Bertarelli and several other Alinghi sailors had extensive experience racing catamarans on the Swiss lakes. "The answer evolved," Drummond says. "Both teams improved hull shapes and other technology and redefined the modern multihull."

Core Builders had been told to prepare for building both a 90-foot monohull and a 90-by-90-foot multihull. As Tim Smyth wrote about the project in *Seahorse* magazine, "As the legal story unfolded we kept our heads down and pondered the best route to keep our options open." What Smyth and his Core Builders co-head, Mark Turner, did was to expand their oven to accommodate a wide, 90-foot monohull, which turned out to be a costly error. When the multihull was the call, they had to live with the huge oven to build all the multihull's narrow elements.

Turner and Smyth had figured it would take 25,000 hours to build the latest version (version 5) of an 80-foot monohull of the sort that had been used in the Cup since 1992. Divide by six months, the time frame to have the boat sailing, and they figured they'd need 22 builders. VPLP and associates had told Core it would take 18 months to build the trimaran they had designed. Given the original

October 2009 date for the DOG match that was on paper in December 2008 when building commenced, Core had just eight months to complete the giant multihull — referred to as *BMW Oracle Racing 90* — to allow time for sailing trials, team practice, and the inevitable modifications. The work force would jump to 70 people recruited from all over the world. "Work permits, accommodations, furniture, schooling, and relocation became as big a part of the job as fiber selection and test panel work," Tim Smyth wrote in *Seahorse*. He says the massive rigging loads on the trimaran and the extra-large appendages (daggerboards, rudders) meant extra-thick laminates. The amount of material Core used to build the trimaran would have been sufficient to build five version-5 yachts.

"Then the design team went off to Valencia and put their heads together and decided we could bring the build program up another two months and launch the boat early July," Smyth says. The memory causes him to put his head in his hands. "The marketing team got all excited — hey, we could launch it on the Fourth of July! We got served up this fait accompli, and at first we believed it. We believed it for ten days until the sheer, ridiculous impossibility of the situation dawned on us. We said no way. That was a big deal for our team. They got a bit of a wobble on. But we had done some soul-searching and realized it wasn't humanly possible to build this thing in six months. The French said 18 months. We were doing it in eight. Now six? No way."

Legal Update – March 8, 2008

New York Supreme Court reaffirms GGYC's status as Challenger of Record, denying motion for re-argument by SNG, and denying motion by SNG to declare GGYC's Notice of Challenge and Certificate to be in non-compliance and invalid under the Deed of Gift.

FEET WET – MONOS

While *BMW Oracle Racing 90* was taking shape in Anacortes, in northwest Washington State, Russell Coutts organized the sailing team to train in both monohulls and multihulls. Quality racing of any sort would suffice to keep the whole team sharp and involved. And the monohull could have been reinstated if an agreement was reached. Anything was possible at this stage. And two premier classes of high-performance boats, TP52s and RC44s, had busy European seasons planned. There was another factor: the multihull campaign in Decision 35 (D35) boats on Lake Garda that Coutts had planned did not come to fruition. BMW Oracle Racing had chartered a boat and was having sails made when it was informed its entry would not be accepted. It seemed Ernesto Bertarelli had intervened with other D35 owners and succeeded in blocking BMW Oracle Racing's participation.

Another factor was that Larry Ellison loved sailing the RC44s. The team owned two of the light, 44-foot monohull "dinghies" conceived by Russell Coutts and co-designed by Coutts and Andrej Justin. The 44s have

Russell Coutts (left) and Larry Ellison checking on progress at Core Builders where their futuristic trimaran is taking shape.

become a popular one-design class in Europe. With a crew weight of 680 kilograms (1496 pounds), the 44s were excellent vehicles for both fleet and match-racing practice for BMW Oracle Racing sailors. Their frightening combination of speed and instability require the concentration and crew coordination levels of a performance multihull. They also functioned, early on, as a platform for relationship-building between sailors. Ellison and Coutts were on one boat as driver and tactician. Jim Spithill and John Kostecki were driver and tactician on the other boat.

"The 44s are so unstable," Ellison told ESPN sailing analyst Gary Jobson in an interview in June, 2008. "After you drive these things, you can't go back to a regular sailboat. We go downwind at 24 knots — 24 knots downwind in a 44-foot monohull in, I don't know, 30 knots of breeze?! If you look at the mast you think you've got the wrong mast on the boat. It's way too big. I mean, what were you thinking, Russell?" Ellison laughs. "The boat is so overpowered. When you think you're going to broach that means you're getting close to the fastest sailing angle. There's maybe a one-to-three-degree separation between maximum speed and a broach."

Ellison says the cockpit of the 44 is where he really got to know his CEO, Russell Coutts. "The first time I ever raced with Russell was in April, 2008, at the Cagliari Cup in Italy," Ellison says. "I had gotten to know Russell in his engineering/leadership role when he was rebuilding our team. He's a very methodical engineer, well-liked, organized, extremely smart. But the second we got into a race, Russell went from calm, cool, collected to just — on the edge. He is so competitive, and he wants to sail so well that if I do anything that's slightly off, he'll yell at me. He's, you know, SMOOTH IT UP LARRY, SMOOTH IT UP! Our trimmer Ross Halcrow told him to stop yelling at me because it was scaring the hell out of me. But it took until the end of the regatta for him to stop yelling at me. And he said, Well that's pretty good, okay, okay, you're okay. He's hyper-competitive. I think that's a common denominator of the really great athletes that I've known."

Jobson: "Is Russell as competitive as you?"

Ellison: "Yeah, easy."

Ellison told me that in his first match-race series in RC44s, it was blowing 22 knots. They blew out a chute and were playing catch-up to a decent Polish team. "Coming to the finish we were both going 18 knots," Ellison told me. "There was about a meter between the boats, we were side by side. It was a port-starboard situation. I bore away a little for the finish, and Russell starts screaming, NO, HIT HIM, HIT HIM! We went screaming across the line, missed the Polish boat by a meter. Turns out he also beat us by a meter. Russell was furious. He looked at me. I TOLD YOU TO HIT HIM! I looked at him calmly and said, It's your boat. Next time I'll hit him. The trimmers, Ross Halcrow and Cheese [Dirk] de Ridder were giving me those looks: yep, he's crazy. Russell's just a little competitive.

"In another regatta, our last race was against the Japanese team that wasn't very good. Russell says okay Larry, we have to beat these guys to win, but no problem, be conservative, drive well but conserve the assets, we're about to put the trophy on the mantle.

BY ROGER VAUGHAN • PAGE 56

I keep away from them in the pre-start, and we get a nice lead, four to five boat lengths. It's pretty breezy so I take a conservative angle downwind. Russell comes over to me and says, What the fuck are you doing? Have you forgotten how to sail? Come up and let's get going. I put on the hairiest angle I could. The Japanese were now 16 lengths behind us. Russell says, That's better. He's out of his mind. Preserve the assets?

"Ashore, he's another person. The guys love him. He's thoughtful, a good leader, a very good engineer who makes well-informed decisions. His thought processes are clear, understandable, disciplined, and he almost always comes up with the right answer. He's as good as our best engineers at Oracle, a remarkable guy. I understand why we lost in New Zealand."

Jimmy Spithill says the many regattas they sailed in the RC44s and the TP52 class were important for bragging rights around camp as well as the training they provided. At that first regatta in Cagliari, Spithill learned that his competition was serious. While Spithill would win the season, Ellison and Coutts won the match-racing portion of that regatta with an 8–1 record. Spithill posted a 7–2.

"It was pretty impressive," Spithill says, "for someone to come in and sail that well in windy conditions. It's hard enough for a pro to do that, let alone someone with Larry's commitments. He jumped on the boat with minimal sailing time and got up to speed quickly. He's a good sailor."

Ellison quips that Spithill is pretty good himself — "for a young guy. But," he says, "anytime you sail with Russell, you have a good chance of winning. But I hate it when he yells at me."

FEET WET – MULTIS

Jim Spithill says the day in December Coutts committed to the multihull he started thinking about finding himself a boat to sail. "The team had a little break over Christmas," Spithill says. "I was in Australia and there was a Formula 18 race on. I rang up my brother-in-law, who sails multis, and asked him to find me a boat. I had a go, pulled the trigger, put my head down and went multihull sailing." As a kid, Spithill had learned to sail on a Hobie 18 his father borrowed from a neighbor. But that was a dim memory. He'd been sailing monohulls ever since. "Initially I didn't give multihulls enough credit," Spithill says. "Like anything else, you shouldn't give an opinion about something unless you've tried it."

When Spithill returned to the team base in Valencia, Mike Drummond was lying in wait for him with his A-Class catamaran. "I dragged him off kicking and screaming," Drummond says. "It was a day when the sea breeze was fully developed, with a steep chop. It was a tough day to sail. The A-Class is a high- performance boat. It's 18 feet long with a 30-foot mast. The total weight of the boat, all up and ready to sail, is 165 pounds. It's the greatest boat I've ever sailed, and a handful the day Jimmy took it out. I watched from the chase boat and had to chuckle. But I was also impressed. The waves were quite big. It was hard not to be washed off the boat going upwind, and difficult to avoid stuffing the bow in downwind. Jimmy's skill and athleticism, his ability to handle the boat in those conditions without damaging it — which I was incredibly relieved about — or without capsizing, was very impressive. I threw him in the deep end and he survived, came through just fine."

Jim Spithill would ultimately win steering rights of USA 17.

As a group, the team quickly jumped into the Extreme 40 (X40) class of catamarans, carbon fiber boats first launched in 2005 that are promoted under a double-A headline, "action, adrenaline." They didn't disappoint. Australia's Glenn Ashby was on hand as a coach for the team's first go-round in the

X40s. Ashby is among the best small multihull sailors in the world, having won seven A-Class world championships, two Tornado world championships, and a silver medal (Tornado, with skipper Darren Bundock) in the Beijing Olympics in 2008.

"Glenn is a freak," Mike Drummond says with a laugh. In Kiwi-speak, that is an ultimate compliment from one A-Class sailor to another. Ashby would disappear into his Olympic campaign after the X40 session, but he would return. Sailors new to multihulls are always concerned about pitchpoling: digging a hull into a wave and flipping stern over bow. "We got that issue out of the way on the first day," Glenn Ashby says with a laugh.

"It was very windy," Spithill recalls, "with an offshore breeze coming off the mountains in Valencia. We were going fast, and there was talk of bearing away. Glenn says no matter what happens you have to commit to it, so round we went, it seemed a bit dodgy, but he said commit, so we committed, and over we went. It turned out the release valve on the hydraulics for the mainsheet wasn't working. We hit it and nothing happened. We laughed about it later on.

"It was a good thing. You have to be able to do that in the smaller boats because it is a way to learn — push it over the edge and see what happens, what it feels like. You do the same thing in dinghies. The 40-footer isn't that small, but it is a size you can push, tip over, and be okay, not hurt the boat or the people. You can't do that with the ORMA 60s."

But the ORMA 60s have to be an essential part of

any multihull learning curve when the goal is a boat nearly twice that size. Because *USA 17* (the renamed *BMW Oracle Racing 90*) began life as a scaled-up version of the ORMA 60 *Groupama*, it made sense to go sail on that very boat. That meant getting together with *Groupama* skipper Franck Cammas, one of the most talented and respected skippers in the ORMA world. Cammas gave up studying piano for racing multihulls, and his success on the water has made it look like a smart move. He won all the ORMA grands prix in 2005 and 2006, has won the ORMA world championship five times, and holds seven passage records, including the record for sailing nonstop around the world for the coveted Jules Verne Trophy (January to March, 2010).

As early as March, 2008, a group of sailors from BMW Oracle Racing organized a trip to Lorient, France, on the Brittany coast, for a two-week training session on Franck Cammas's *Groupama 2*, the inshore racing trimaran (*Groupama 3* is configured for racing offshore). Among the afterguard were Russell Coutts, James Spithill, and American John Kostecki, who has been with BMW Oracle Racing since 2003 as tactician. A member of four different America's Cup syndicates, Kostecki had left BMW Oracle Racing in 2005 when the afterguard infighting became intolerable. BMW Oracle Racing invited him back after the conclusion of America's Cup XXXII, and he quickly accepted.

Kostecki started his sailing career by winning the Sears Cup at age 17, followed by the Sunfish world championship when he was 18 (he was second in the J24 worlds that year). He won a silver medal in the Soling class in the 1988 Olympics, and won the Volvo Round the World Race as skipper of *Illbruck* in 2001–02. With his win as tactician aboard *USA 17*, Kostecki

Tactician John Kostecki (right) with Franck Cammas (at helm) and designer Michel Kermarec on board an ORMA 60.

is the only sailor ever to win an Olympic medal, the Round the World Race, and an America's Cup.

In the 1990s, Kostecki had raced a 40-foot catamaran in San Francisco prepping for Pro-Sail, a short-lived series of catamaran regattas in the United States designed for a live audience. And Kostecki was Spithill's regular tactician in Extreme 40 sessions. But *Groupama 2* makes the X40s look like dinghies, and it was the first trimaran the BMW Oracle Racing group had sailed.

BMW Oracle Racing sailors arrived in Lorient just two days after their counterparts from Alinghi had finished a training session in an ORMA 60. On their last day on the water, the Alinghi sailors had capsized the big boat, breaking the mast and injuring several of the crew. When the BMW Oracle Racing sailors arrived at their hotel, one of the injured Alinghi crew had been released from the hospital, and happened to be checking out. "We had a chance to chat with him," Kostecki says. "It was a bit daunting to see the cuts and bruises before we even took to the water. We thought, oh boy, what are we getting into. We took our foot off the gas pedal. Franck was also conservative. He didn't want to wreck his program."

On BMW Oracle Racing's first day on *Groupama 2*, it was blowing 25 knots with big seas. Small sails were raised, and the boat still felt over-canvassed, hitting 30 knots of boat speed more than once. "It was very similar to Volvo sailing," Kostecki says. "You're going very fast, and you are constantly wet." For two weeks BMW Oracle Racing's monohull sailors learned the ropes, then had some match racing against another ORMA 60, *Banque Populaire*. Kostecki called tactics for Franck Cammas. He echoes Glenn Ashby's perception about having to make strategic plans much further ahead than on a monohull. "Because of the increased speed," Kostecki says, "you have to make faster decisions, and count on your skipper to execute them."

Legal Update – April 14, 2008

SNG files an appeal in Appellate Division challenging the Supreme Court's decision of March 17, 2008, that invalidated CNEV, and named GGYC as the Challenger of Record for America's Cup XXXIII.

An excerpt from GGYC's comment regarding the appeal: "The decision to go to the appellate court also contradicts previous and repeated assurances given by senior Alinghi team members and lawyers to the sailing community that they would not appeal."

Legal Update – May 12, 2008

The New York Supreme Court issued an order (based on its judgment of November 27, 2007) that the next America's Cup match should take place in ten months (March, 2009), and that the Defender should disclose the venue six months prior to that.

Alinghi's appeal of April 14, 2008 was pending.

COMPETITION

Looking back at the schedule of racing planned, one wonders how the sailors made it from one regatta to the next in time for the start. Kostecki and eight other BMW Oracle Racing sailors were racing in the TP52 class (they placed 2nd in the MedCup). Coutts, Ellison, Spithill, and full crews were racing RC44s. And all of them were still beating each other's brains out in the X40s. The luffing match between Jim Spithill and Franck Cammas is a case in point. A nine-race, in-house match-race battle between Spithill, on one boat, and Cammas and Coutts, on the other boat, was the highlight of the week of March 17, 2008.

Jim Spithill is a charming guy who handles himself as well as any 31-year-old rock-star sailor you will ever meet. He's friendly, engaging. He's a good listener, comfortable to be around, with the easy, delighted laugh of a kid half his age. Spithill often speaks graciously about people who have helped him along the way, and about working together with people vying for the same job for the good of the team. But this is also the guy who, at 22 years old, took his mentor, the crusty Australian yachtsman Syd Fisher, to court . . . and won. "He respected me for it," Spithill says. "The biggest lesson I learned from Syd was not to lie down and let someone walk on you." Syd included. Make no mistake, James Spithill is a competitor. As Larry Ellison said of Coutts, once on a boat, Spithill undergoes a transformation into a hyper-focused athlete with only one thing — success — on his mind. That was evident in the last race of the in-house battle in X40s.

When Spithill is reminded that the race ended in a capsize, he laughed. "Oh yeah, with Franck. We luffed him, and over he went. The best part was that

Jim Spithill (left) and Russell Coutts in a reflective moment.

Russell was on board as well." Spithill laughed again. He couldn't help himself. "And Tim Jeffery [BMW Oracle Racing's communications director], he was on board that day." Another laugh.

"We were having an awesome match-race series with Franck," Spithill says. "It was a picture-perfect day off Valencia, with the breeze building to 16 knots. It was the final race on the final day, Friday, of a weeklong session. It was all on. We were leading, but we had a penalty, and had to get rid of it. We were trying to create something to offset the penalty, engage Franck on the run, which we successfully did. Franck tried to go over the top of us, so we luffed him. He sailed up too high, and went over.

"It was good, we were learning about multihulls, Franck was learning the match-racing side. We were all learning a heap. We didn't want them to tip over, but we all learned from it and were open with each other. At the end we all had a beer together. There was a good feeling in the group." Spithill laughs. "We got some great photos of the event we still love to show to those guys. We had one blown up and put on the office wall."

One of Spithill's biggest fans is Larry Ellison. "The first time I sailed against Jimmy was on San Francisco Bay," Ellison says. "I lost every race. I didn't want to go out the next day. I thought maybe I should quit sailing. In my defense I hadn't sailed in a while, and Jimmy was on the match-race circuit. He hadn't lost a race all year, and he sure wasn't going to lose to me. By the third day I had won a couple races. The score was 17–3 or something. I had been racing pretty well against the pros, but he killed me. Horrible. I was distraught. Russell comes over and says to me, Aren't you glad he's on our team?" Ellison howls with laughter.

Later on Coutts would say that if America's Cup XXXIII had been raced in October, 2008, as originally ordained by the court, Franck Cammas would probably have steered the boat. "Spithill wouldn't have had the time to prepare," Coutts says. "But as Jimmy got more time in the boat he was clearly the best guy." Spithill knew that Cammas was, by consensus, the fastest gun in the big multihulls. As such, he was fair game. Because the race date had been moved ahead five months to March, 2009, time was on Spithill's side, and he was making his move. To win the America's Cup, first he had to beat out Franck Cammas for the helm.

RAMPING UP

The summer of 2008 was full on. Seventy builders were working 60 to 65 hour weeks creating *USA 17* — hull, floats, appendages, and mast. One of many curveballs thrown at the builders was the task of making a spare set of floats. There was concern that since the first testing of the boat would be in Fidalgo Bay (southeast of Vancouver Island), the boat might encounter one of the logs that typically float around in those waters. Another set of floats? No problem. They're only 115 feet long.

Curveballs arrived regularly in Anacortes. "When the legal battle resulted in the date being pushed back," Tim Smyth says, "the design team would have time to make changes. We were building a boat compromised for an earlier regatta, so when the regatta date was moved ahead we had to re-optimize the boat given the added time available. This caused either a rework, or we'd tear something up and start again, or we'd just have to stop what we were doing and chuck it in the bin."

Mike Drummond says the redesign process started even before the team knew it had additional time. "Our guys spent a lot of time considering what they would do if they were Alinghi," Drummond says. "The conclusion was that Alinghi would have the best chance by going for light air. And (according to the Deed of Gift) as Defender, they got to chose the venue. The minute we finished the design of *USA 17* we knew we had to revisit it, improve its performance in light conditions. When you ask designers to come up with a boat that can handle anything, as we did initially, they have to take into account strong winds and waves. So initially *USA 17* wasn't at all suited to performing in light wind."

Core Builder's original intention was to subcontract a portion of the work in the interest of meeting the oppressive deadline. But Smyth and Turner concluded that other builders they contacted didn't have the wherewithal or the resources to deliver on time — or, perhaps, the motivation. All the parts of *USA 17* were so enormous that the sequence of building was critical. If progress got out of sequence, parts would

Following pages: Design team members Claudio Cairoli (squatting) and Manolo Luiz de Elvira testing an early model in a wind tunnel.

have to be stored outside until they were needed. There wasn't room in the shops. "If subcontractors missed the timing," Smyth says, "we'd be stuck. We concluded we'd have to do it ourselves." Hall Spars, in Bristol, Rhode Island, was an exception. Hall built all three masts for the soft sails.

The sailing team was equally engaged, although they might have been having a bit more fun. Ellison and Coutts were on a roll in the RC44 series, winning the City of Marseilles Cup in June, and the Malcesine Cup on Lake Garda in July. Frank Cammas won the 500-boat Bol d'Or regatta on Lake Geneva in a D35 catamaran, and Spithill and crew won the Jaeger-Le-Coultre "Just the Best" regatta in X40 catamarans in Italy. Spithill and crew also won the Chicago–Mackinac race in July.

Then there would be a setback. In a split (3–2) decision, the COR appeal filed by Alinghi on May 15 was decided in Alinghi's favor. CNEV had been reinstated as COR.

Legal Update – July 29, 2008

"Accordingly, the orders of the Supreme Court, New York County (Herman Cahn, J.), entered March 18, 2008, which, inter alia, declared CNEV's challenge invalid and GGYC the Challenger of Record under the Deed of Gift, should be reversed, on the law, with costs, CNEV declared the Challenger of Record, and, in keeping with the Deed of Gift's requirement that the

defender be given at least 10 months' written notice to prepare for the challenge, the 10-month period should be tolled until service of a copy of this order."

Legal Update – July 31, 2008

GGYC files an appeal with the Court of Appeals. "We believe the Challenger of Record has to be a real yacht club," says GGYC spokesman Tom Ehman. "It cannot be something that is manufactured with a defender to set up a one-sided event. This decision would set an absurd precedent."

MANAGING

Russell Coutts says that Larry Ellison was totally involved in the management of the team for America's Cup XXXIII. "We were on the phone weekly," Coutts says. "Larry was in on all the strategic decisions. He also got all the performance information, all the data. He obviously has a lot of technical savvy, and he had good input. He was able to cut through all the information that can be very confusing, and simplify it."

Both the groundbreaking nature of the boat and the advancement of technology made this Cup extra confusing for those analyzing data. As Ian Burns points out, "In previous Cups you had 100 variables providing readouts every second; a megabyte of data per day. In 2010, we had 150 to 200 channels processing 2000 to 3000 variables ten times every second. We were keeping tabs on things never designed before. All existing systems struggled with the amount of data we were collecting."

Many new systems were designed, right down to wind instruments that hadn't advanced significantly in years. BMW Oracle Racing engineers redesigned the wind vane, added a high-resolution sensor, and arrived at a wind angle measurement accurate to .02 degrees, 100 times more accurate than what is available off the shelf. The rebuilt vane also had improved frequency and inertia control, so it wouldn't swing back and forth when the boat heeled or pitched.

Ellison made the first of several key decisions after GGYC lost its recognition as Challenger of Record in Appellate Court. He chose to keep going full-tilt in all directions. He served notice to designers, builders, and sailors that all the lights remained green.

"That was a really big decision," Coutts says. "Larry felt we would win our appeal, and we carried on. But at that point we were out of the Cup. It was a financial risk, for sure. What made Larry's decision carry even more weight was that Alinghi stopped work after they won the Challenger of Record reversal. They thought they would win in court and have us dismissed. While we kept going, they mothballed their boat and stopped work. That was a big mistake. By the time we won the final appeal, we had made a lot of progress."

When asked why he would take such a risk, why he would keep the lights on after having been ousted as Challenger of Record, Ellison pauses, takes a breath. "I have a problem," he says. "Once I start competing for something, I have a hard time giving up. That can be a virtue, and that can be a curse. I just couldn't stop the process once I had set the goal of winning the Cup. Every setback became a learning experience — let's do things better, let's not make the same mistakes we did the last time."

As CEO, Coutts ran a very open campaign within the camp. Veterans of previous Cup syndicates were surprised at the lack of secrecy and the availability of information, including, in many cases, budgets. In the cloak-and-dagger business of an America's Cup, this approach was a breath of fresh air.

"Many people worry about information leaks to competitors," Coutts says. "I see it as more of a gain even if some information does leak, because you end up with a more efficient structure. People are more motivated because they know what's going on and understand why they are doing things. The benefits far outweigh the slight loss of security."

One had to wonder how Coutts managed the star-studded group around him that read like an international Who's Who in sailing, yacht design and technology, and yacht building. There were enough people walking around with Olympic medals and

Following pages: On August 22, 2008, in Anacortes, Washington, Melina Erkelens, who was with Oracle Racing from the outset, christens BMW Oracle 90. *The boat would later be renamed* USA 17 *as a more manageable name for the Cup.*

world championship titles to sink the proverbial ship. Coutts's own shelf full of medals wasn't too shabby, probably on the top of the heap, or close to it, and that certainly lent credibility to his leadership. But he says there were no runaway egos. "Good people usually understand what they don't know," Coutts says. "Our group had widely diverse opinions on some topics, and that led to healthy debate, which was one of our strengths."

Tom Ehman loves to refer to Coutts as a "leader of men and women." "No one worked harder than Russell," Ehman says. "If there was a win along the way, no one was more fired up than Russell. He'd be so excited it was infectious. He'd make a few calls and pretty soon the wine was flowing and there was dinner for 100 people. He was like a kid. I've also seen him angry and disappointed, but in those moments he'd take the hit and get on with it."

COMPROMISE BOAT

USA 17 rolled out of its purpose-built shed in Anacortes on August 22, 2008. Core had completed the job in just nine months, an amazing accomplishment given the amount of re-direction required along the way. After three days of static load tests on the hard, Melinda Erkelens smacked a bottle of champagne into the end of the bowsprit (risky business, as we shall see), and christened the boat BMW Oracle 90. For the Cup it would

Reefed in light air, BMW Oracle 90*'s initial outing in Fidalgo Bay, off Anacortes, Washington, showed a wary approach.*

be changed to the more manageable *USA 17,* which was a nod to the late Tom Blackaller, San Francisco Bay sailor extraordinaire, whose boat was named *USA* for the 1987 America's Cup campaign in Fremantle, Australia. Then the boat was lowered into Fidalgo Bay, off Puget Sound, in front of Core Builders.

On September 1, the 6,500 square foot mains'l was raised up the 50.2-meter (164 feet, 8 inches off the deck) mast for the first time, and the boat went

Left: BMW Oracle 90's *beam nearly matched its length over-all. Top: Ian "Fresh" Burns (middle) and his performance team analyzed data from more than 250 sensors located all over the boat. Bottom: A worker at Core Builders inside one of the boat's 115-foot floats.*

BY ROGER VAUGHAN • PAGE 81

sailing. The sails had been built by Craig Phillips and a crew of 12 sailmakers at the Oracle Racing, Inc., loft in Minden, Nevada, near the North Sails 3DL/3Di plant. North would manufacture the sail blanks on its molds, and truck them over to Oracle Racing, Inc., for finishing. "We lucked into a great facility," says Phillips, who was working on producing America's Cup sails for the seventh time (he started with *Kookaburra* in Australia in 1984). "We could lay out a gennaker with a 70-meter (230-foot) luff length on our floor," Phillips says. "The gennakers were 8,500 square feet. We needed a dozen guys in the loft because the sails were so heavy. You needed a guy behind you and a guy in front of you to pull the work through the sewing machine."

Russell Coutts's understatement prior to casting off for the first time that he found the boat "incredibly challenging" drew smiles from his teammates. He said they would proceed "conservatively." A photograph taken that day by team photographer Gilles Martin-Raget shows the boat with a reefed mains'l in 6 to 8 knots of wind. That is conservative.

While the boat was being sailed off Anacortes for two weeks, and Ian Burns and his performance team were collecting data from more than 250 sensors covering all areas of the boat from rudders to sails, including fiber-optic sensors built into the carbon-fiber structure, Mike Drummond and the design team continued to reconfigure the trimaran for light air.

"We were considering different appendages," Drummond says, "and a taller rig. But the first change was new floats, longer, and with an improved shape for lower drag. Hervé Devaux tweaked the structures, so while the floats were bigger they were not heavier. At the same time we were running analyses on appendage configurations. The boat that was launched had a daggerboard and rudder on the central hull. There were smaller rudders on the floats, and small, curved foils to provide lift. We settled on large, curved daggerboards — dagger foils we called them — on the floats, with no board on the central hull. Michel Kermarec lived and breathed the appendage development."

"There was talk for some time of building a completely new boat," Tim Smyth says, "and using the first one for practice. The idea was to take the boat to Valencia as soon as possible since the regatta would be there. But sending a totally compromised boat that needed development to Valencia wouldn't work because by the rule, the boat had to be built here. Once in Valencia you couldn't even change a rudder. A new boat was the plan for a long time. But there simply wasn't enough time. We started by building new floats."

"It took us a lot of analysis to arrive at the right position and shape for the appendages," Mike Drummond says. "By the time we had the confidence to proceed with them, the floats were already under construction. It was a difficult boat-building job to make them fit."

"We had to rework the floats," Smyth says. "One of them was already joined, complete, with a very nice paint finish. Having to cut that open was depressing. For builders you can imagine the job, a 115-foot long, narrow thing a small man can only crouch inside that has heaps of bulkheads. Having dagger foils meant the load on the floats would be 30 percent higher, so we had to go back in, rip out the inside skin, put in core reinforcement, add extra layers inside and out, and rework them.

"The dagger foil design wasn't finished," Smyth says. "Those were Mark Turner's babies, and would require a superhuman effort to build. At 20 feet long, six inches thick where they exit the floats, and three feet wide, they would have to sustain a 90-ton side load at the floats. The structural combination was impressive. Titanium, high-strength steel, autoclaved carbon, and exotic plastics came together to encase this huge dagger foil that had to swivel and slide under load and be controlled from a safe distance. And there were two sets, one for the upwind-downwind course of Race 1; the other set was more curved for reaching around the triangular course of Race 2. They were very difficult to engineer to make them light and strong enough, and very hard, and expensive, to build. I know Alinghi built ten daggerboards before they got four that didn't break. The floats would be finished and on the boat, sailing, before we got those things done. It's stressful to recall those days."

"My name was mud with Tim, that's for sure," Mike Drummond says. "But in the end it was do we lose, or do we win? If we put the new appendage configuration on, it was so much faster in light air that we had a chance. If we hadn't done it, I was confident we would lose in light air. The margins I'm talking about, in less than 7 knots of wind, are big. On VPP, the new appendages were worth something like 40 minutes around the course, roughly speaking. It was a chance we had to take."

SAN DIEGO

USA 17 and all its various parts were craned onto a barge on September 26, 2008, for the week-long trip down the Pacific Coast to San Diego. The plan, as Peter Rush reported in his frequent news blog on bmworacleracing.com, was to be in San Diego for a two-month training session before the whole show was shipped to Valencia. As it turned out, San Diego would be home to the syndicate for 14 months, a situation that wreaked havoc with the domestic situations of the many BMW Oracle Racing employees who had taken up residence in Valencia. And while the "temporary" base camp at the Convention Center (the very same patch of asphalt Dennis Conner used in the 1988, 1992, and 1995 Stars & Stripes campaigns), and less-than-convenient accommodations would have sufficed for two months, they wore very thin over 14 months — especially after the giant wingsail made its entrance. But from training, preparation, and boat-modification standpoints, San Diego turned out to be a handy stopover. It is an active port and a good sailing location, the weather is pleasant, there are good restaurants, there's a great zoo, even a dog beach. And, while located 1,000 miles south of Anacortes, it is at least on the same continental coast as Core Builders, who were constantly making modifications and delivering parts.

Tom Ehman's logic was, as usual, irrefutable: "There was no point in going anywhere until we knew where we were going." The venue for AC XXXIII was up in the air until GGYC's appeal was finally decided by the New York courts in December, 2009. All in all, fetching up in San Diego was good luck.

Also in September, 2008, Mike Drummond very quietly made an initial move that would have great impact on the campaign. He asked Dave Hubbard to do some thinking about a hard wingsail for *USA 17*. An engineer from MIT, Hubbard has been designing and sailing C-Class catamarans since the 1960s. He designed his first successful wingsail in 1971 for a C-Class boat, and designed a wing in 1973 with two elements that was the essence of his wingsail design for Cup-winning *Stars & Stripes*, the catamaran, in 1988.

Drummond says the wing was part of the light-air theme he was pursuing. But he had no one he could spare to put on the project. "I discussed the concept with Dave," Drummond says. "We started very slowly, before we even knew we had time to build a wingsail. But we knew a wing would be efficient in light wind. *Stars & Stripes* had proved that."

Work on modifying the big trimaran for light air was the number-one priority. The bow was lengthened — a massive job — to accommodate larger headsails. The bowsprit was lengthened to support bigger gennakers for use when not sailing upwind. The only problem was how to support the bowsprit. Bowsprits traditionally rely on bows deep enough to provide a wide angle for a bobstay that holds the bowsprit down against the heavy upward pressure of sails and rigging that are tacked to it. A "dolphin striker," a spreader-like rod protruding toward the water from where bowsprit meets bow, helps improve the bobstay angle and provide strength. But the bow of *USA 17* wasn't very deep. As a result, the bowsprit project was among the most difficult problems the design team and the builders had to solve.

"The whole bowsprit saga is quite a story," Tim Smyth says. "We botched it thoroughly. Alinghi thought we never used it because our system was so good we were keeping it a secret. The reality was that it was so useless and such a screw-up that we couldn't use it. I don't think the sailors jibed the boat four times during the 14 months we were in San Diego."

Mark Turner says he lost count of how many bowsprits were built. "I think the first time we succeeded in keeping it attached to the boat for any amount of time was in Valencia, a week before the Cup," he says.

"We even lost one of them at the dock, while pre-tensioning the rig," Scott Ferguson (BMW Oracle Racing's rig designer) says with a rueful chuckle. "Mike was pushing to get more sail area, and we were trying to double the length of the bowsprit. The loads went up quite a bit. It took

a while to get to the bottom of it." Luckily, the day Melinda Erkelens hauled off and smacked the bowsprit with a bottle of champagne, the troublesome spar stayed together.

Once in San Diego, Jim Spithill personally took on the removal of the big rudder from the main hull of the boat. "Mike and Russell were against removing it," Spithill says, "and Franck and the French guys never thought we could get rid of it and still have control bearing away. But I figured you have to get rid of some of these luxuries to make a gain in boat speed. You'll somehow just figure out how to sail the boat. We'd still be able to tack. It wouldn't be as easy, but we could do it. You have to remember when the boat is upright, the float rudders are half out of water."

One day in San Diego, Spithill asked one of the shore crew to cut the rudder in half. "We had two of them," Spithill says, "so I figured even if I buggered it up we have a spare. We went sailing and it wasn't bad, so we cut more off it. Finally I said we should just take it off. Mike and Russell came back and saw what we had done, and that it was working okay. I think a lot of us had that attitude of just taking things on and pushing as hard as we could, without being stupid and ruining the campaign."

Russell Coutts applauded that kind of initiative.

Not having the rudder on the main hull would haunt Spithill in Race 1, but only for a minute or so.

A Core Builders' worker inside one of the soft-sail masts, sorting out the maze of halyards leading aloft.

The mast also kept getting longer. Again, the original design was for a conservative, all-around boat that was initially expected to race three months after it was launched. With the venue unknown, and to be chosen by Alinghi, that could possibly be in heavy wind and seas. The mast was super safe and heavy compared to what evolved. With more knowledge, more time, more experience sailing the boat, and a good bet that Alinghi was tuning for light air, the mast grew faster than bamboo.

"I remember one meeting early on when we were talking mast heights," Jim Spithill says, "and it was a big, heavily debated decision to go to 50 meters. Frank and the French guys were really worried. Someone mentioned a 60-meter mast as a joke, and everyone just laughed. You wouldn't even consider it."

But the designers went for it, and launched the boat with a 50-meter mast. After the first day of sailing off Anacortes, trimmer Dirk de Ridder remembers talking to fellow-trimmer Ross Halcrow about how it all had felt. "We'd been told the boat was going to be extremely overpowered with a 50-meter mast," de Ridder says, "that it was dangerously high. After sailing that first time we were saying it didn't feel dangerous at all, or close to the edge."

Mast 2 started at 55.3 meters (181 feet, 5 inches). An addition during construction made it 58.8 meters (192 feet, 9 inches). It went into the boat in October, 2008, for the first set of trials in San Diego. Again, there was no feeling of being overpowered. Mast 3, at 60.8 meters (199 feet, 4 inches) was begun almost immediately. Mast 3 was lengthened to 66.3 meters (217 feet, 5 inches) while under construction.

TAMING "THE BEAST"

It didn't take long for the sailors to begin referring to their big tri as "The Beast." The media were calling it Dog-Zilla, a play on the acronym for "Deed of Gift." Everything about it was big, heavy, beastly. Today's computerized design tools will tell you everything you want to know about a boat's performance in all conditions and configurations, so while the data that registered about loading revealed no surprises, the numbers were sobering when they represented larger-than-life-size realities sailors had to contend with, hands-on. There was a 75-ton compression load on the mast step; 32 tons on the forestay with the mainsail sheeted on; 24 tons on the mainsheet. The wingsail would tame that to 4 tons.

Bowman Brad Webb, who previously sailed with TAG Heuer in 1995 and America True in 2000 before joining the original Oracle team for the 2003 Cup match, said the first day they sailed in Anacortes they had five jibs on the boat and a crew of 16. "Things were heavy and hard," Webb says. "Sails weighed around 300 to 400 kilos each [660 to 880 pounds]. It took five people to move them. We craned them on board at the dock, and used halyards to move them to and from chase boats."

Joey Newton, who worked the mid-deck, had the job of getting sails aboard before leaving the dock. He says it was a huge logistical operation just getting off the dock. "It wasn't like a normal boat where you can grab five guys and pick up the main," Newton says. "We needed cranes, and special booms to pick up the sails. Just to put the cable in the luff of a gennaker we had to get a 10-ton truck and two forklifts to get enough tension on it, then get the sail coiled and lashed up on the dock. Getting sails on board in the morning while other guys were busy at their jobs on the boat at the same time was dangerous. I had horrible thoughts of halyards or clips breaking."

For several months, the whole crew sailed wearing hard hats and life jackets. "I was terrified on a daily basis," Brad Webb says. "The first day when we did load testing we had stuff falling out of the sky and missing people. In San Diego we had blocks tearing off the deck and strops breaking. There was always something breaking. As much engineering as there was in the boat, it was on the hairy edge. It's the most extreme sailing craft ever put on the water. After a while, we got used to what might break, what looked right and what didn't, where you could stand at any given time and be safe. So we finally got rid of the hats and jackets to reduce weight and windage. But we still couldn't account for surprises."

Adjusting the leech line. Crewmen were happy to wear hard hats and life vests in the early days when things kept breaking.

John Kostecki says "terrifying" is the right word. "Let me put it this way," Kostecki says, "I was more scared on this boat than I was at any time during the Volvo Race. It wasn't just a little scary, it was scary. We had great designers, great engineers, great sailors all coming up with a boat that was changed radically along the way, everything was as light as possible, it was incredibly loaded, there were unknowns here and there, we didn't know how hard to push, and we only had a certain amount of time with the new design configurations . . . Yes, it was scary."

The boat had four positions on the mast for headsails. Each position had two halyards, one for a designated forestay for the sail, the other for the sail. During the weeks of testing, a sail change could take an hour. "We'd start out by hoisting a genoa," Brad Webb says. "Then they would call for the next sail down we named the Solent. We'd drop the jib, take the headstay off the lock and lower it. Then we'd use the halyard to put the sail on the chase boat, hoist the Solent aboard, hoist the Solent forestay into place and lock it, then hoist the Solent."

They experimented with sails with old-fashioned hanks, and discarded that idea. "Hanks were a nightmare," Webb says. "If we couldn't keep the sails on the net — with 45 knots of wind across the deck — and they went overboard while we were going 25 knots, we'd never get them back." They tried jack lines, and those didn't work either.

The netting that spanned the water between main hull and floats would eventually disappear. In

October, 2008, longtime Cup sailor and ocean-racing veteran Matt Mason would conduct a one-man operation to lighten ship. He removed more than 900 kilograms of gear he deemed non-essential. The safety netting was one of the first things to go. Mason would later join the boat's crew, and have to watch his step like everyone else.

Jim Spithill, standing on his helm platform attached to the windward end of the aft beam, was often 10 to 15 meters (35 to 50 feet) above the water. His safety rail disappeared in Mason's "non-essential" purge. "It was like being in a hurricane up there," Spithill says. "Sailing in 15 to 20 knots of wind (true), and with 25 to 35 knots of boat speed, I was standing in 40 to 50 knots of apparent wind all day. It drained my energy. It would weather you. And I couldn't hear a thing. That's why we all wore headsets.

"My biggest job was keeping track of the loads. I had a heads-up display in my sunglasses, like a fighter pilot has on his canopy. Wearing them was difficult to get used to. I walked into a couple posts on the dock. But I got used to it. We were always on the edge, sailing at 100 percent all the time. We had a dozen alarms on the various sensors that were everywhere — forestay, backstays, daggerboards — and they were constantly tripping. The alarms drove everyone crazy. I was watching everything and passing the word, crank on that, ease this, all the time. We also constantly monitored weight to windward, because we had a righting moment to live by. It all came down to how close to the edge you wanted to get, how much you wanted to eat into the safety factors."

Larry Ellison agrees the boat was terrifying: "At least initially, with the soft sails, when I first drove it. It had [bicycle] chains coming off the wheel, and there was no feel, no rim load. It didn't feel like sailing to me at all. I had to learn how to sail again. I watched Jimmy drive. When he wanted to head up he would throw the helm over hard and skid the boat sideways, then straighten it out, and repeat the process — helm over, skid, straighten out — until he had his new course. It was like drifting a car around a corner.

"I learned to drive it by heel angle. I watched the middle hull. If it was lifting a little too fast, I'd head up; if it was falling too fast I'd head off. Heel angle and the speedo are the two things I watched when steering, and you could get into the rhythm of it."

Jim Spithill likes the edge. He rides motorcycles, kitesurfs, and boardsails for fun. The day the wingsail was given the go-ahead, Spithill began taking flying lessons. It seemed appropriate. When he learned about the edge factor in multihulls, his interest was piqued. Glenn Ashby, who returned to BMW Oracle Racing full time in February, 2009, after winning his Olympic silver medal, drove that point home. "I liken multihull sailing to Formula 1," Ashby says. "The guys who do the best are the ones who can keep the pedal down hardest and longest. If you don't push hard, the penalty in boat-speed loss is great. You don't lose a tenth of a knot, like you do in a monohull. You lose two to four knots. You have to sail accurately, on the edge, achieve maximum performance at all times. All the design and technology is of no use if you are only sailing at 80 percent."

Wearing a backpack full of electronics, helmsman Jim Spithill is ready for a day of sailing. Preceeding pages: "The Beast"

Spithill says that early on in training camp he had a conversation with another multihull champion who had stopped by to sail with the team — Roman Hagara from Austria. Hagara has won gold medals in the Tornado in both the Sydney (2000) and Athens

(2004) Olympics, and two Tornado world championships. "We were talking one day before racing," Spithill says, "and it was pretty windy. I remarked that sailing on days like this must feel dangerous. And Romy said yeah, any time you want to be fast on a day like this you've got to be dangerous. You've got to be on the edge. I'll never forget that because he and Glenn were going on about it."

Brad Webb wasn't on board the day the bowsprit broke for the first time, late in 2008. "It spooked the guys," Webb says. "We broke it several times, and realized we had an inherent problem. I stayed well away from it. I never went out on it when we were under load. If I had to make an adjustment, we'd bear away, unload, and I'd go out. We were good about that in all areas. We never put anyone in danger. We unloaded first, got the job done, and loaded back up."

Everyone on board realized this user-friendly system of unloading could not be applied during an actual race.

Another question about race-readiness had to do with the physical challenge the boat presented to the grinders, historically those National Football League linebacker types who man the large-diameter pedestal-driven winches. USA 17's eight grinders were impressive physical specimens in addition to being good sailors. They lived in the gym, and all of them could bench press small cars. But at his peak, a top-ranked grinder can generate one-quarter horsepower for about 60 seconds. Four grinders are sufficient on most "normal" big boats. But on The Beast, with all eight men putting out full effort on four interconnected pedestals, producing a total of two horsepower, it was taking three minutes before the mainsail was fully trimmed after a tack. The long delay getting the main in was causing Jim Spithill to drive very creatively to keep speed up until he could once again reach the upwind targets. That was just another problem that would have to be solved before race day.

Legal Update – April 2, 2009

The decision of the Appellate Division reinstating CNEV as Challenger of Record is overturned by the Court of Appeals: "Since CNEV has failed to show that at the time it submitted its Notice of Challenge it was a 'club fulfilling all the conditions required by' the Deed of Gift, it does not qualify as the Challenger of Record for the 33rd America's Cup competition. The Supreme Court was correct in declaring GGYC to be the valid Challenger of Record."

Legal Update – April 7, 2009

The Supreme Court of New York files an order re-affirming GGYC as Challenger of Record, and setting a date for America's Cup XXXIII ten calendar months from the date of the order, or February, 2010.

THE WINGSAIL

Two days after GGYC was officially (and irrefutably, the appeals process having been exhausted) reinstated as COR, Larry Ellison gave his team the green light to begin building the wingsail. That turned out to be a critical decision. On the defender's side, Alinghi designers pushed for a wing and were told it was too costly.

Ellison says that decision was easy. "The wing is more efficient than any soft sail," Ellison says. "That's easy for designers to calculate. The critical part is that the wing is more reliable. The loading on the mainsheet of the soft sail is astonishing. The wing has no sheet, just a traveler, with loading an order of magnitude lower. The wing would generate more lift, more power with less loading, with a reduced likelihood of breaking, and it could be trimmed much faster. With the wing we'd have a more reliable, faster boat. Also it was obvious all along that *Alinghi* was going into a light-wind speed corner of just three to four knots. Their ideal scenario was to start in seven knots and hope for the wind to die. A wing is so much better in a light-wind situation."

Dave Hubbard's preliminary work on the wingsail began with the wing he had designed for Dennis Conner's catamaran in 1988. As in 1988, Hubbard envisioned a two-element structure. The forward element was a solid wingspar containing the structure that served as the mast and had a leading-edge "nose cone" fairing from top to bottom. A second

Top: Mast designer Scott Ferguson. Bottom: Wingsail designers Dave Hubbard (left), and Joseph Ozanne. Following pages: The wingsail under construction at Core Builders.

vertical element, that began half way to the wing's trailing edge, consisted of movable flaps that could be trimmed individually.

Hubbard had been joined by Joseph Ozanne in December, 2008. Ozanne, a sailor whose degree work was in aeronautical engineering and aerodynamics, had worked on appendages and VPPs for Oracle in the previous campaign. In this campaign he was in charge of developing a dynamic simulator for VPP, until Mike Drummond put him on the wing design. Ozanne says his team had about four months to come up with a concept and sizing. He says there was a bit more time for the structural side of it.

"Mike Drummond was a strong believer," Ozanne says. "Mike pushed hard. I always thought it would be great, but the wing was a crazy project. No one took it very seriously at first. There were strong opinions inside the team. But it was a designer's dream. Big excitement. At every stage of the program, after every presentation I was convinced there was every good reason to stop the project. Because on paper the wing looked really scary. We would ask the builders what are we going to do — is it feasible? And they said sure, no problem, it just takes time. I was surprised how they reacted. No problem.

"The structures guys said no problem. Everybody said it's feasible. The black area was logistics, how to handle it. Mike said just design it and don't worry. Because the logistics were a nightmare."

Rhode Islander Scott Ferguson, whose specialty is designing monohull racing spars for the likes of Volvo 70s and TP52s — he also happens to have won back-to-back Laser Masters championships (2009, 2010) — was manager of the structural-design team.

"I acted as group leader," Ferguson says, "to keep things moving, making decisions about the direction we were headed, how the wing would get rigged, and how the mechanical parts worked together."

Ferguson says he had a wing work group that met once a week. "There were five or six of us around the table and connected by phone. That included Tim Smyth, who had a lot to do with the design as well as the construction of the wing. Dave Hubbard was my touchstone. I always wanted his basic approval about whether or not something would work. He often disagreed or was unsure on a number of design features based on his experience, or some hand calculations. He didn't have finite element tools [cutting-edge software for structural design and analysis] at his disposal like the rest of us, just good sound logic, experience with previous wings, and sketches and drawings to illustrate his ideas. Dave kept our thinking in line, didn't let us get out of control, or get too fancy with the systems we were devising. The system for how the flaps operated essentially came from the *Stars & Stripes* concept. We scaled stuff up, had different hinge points and positions, but lots of systems were fairly similar. The two wings ended up very close in concept."

Hubbard says at the end, he produced same-scale drawings of the two wings, laid them on top of one another, and was quite amazed at how close they were. "I was the guy from the Stone Age with experience," Hubbard says with a grin. "The other guys were space-age with amazing ability. There was a nice merger among us, with lots of respect exchanged."

The basic design concept of the wing was that the various parts would hang on a large, central spar. While other details were being worked out, that gave Core Builders a place to start. "We built the main spar in one 55-meter-long (180-foot) piece, short of full height," Tim Smyth wrote in *Seahorse* magazine. "It had six overlapped joints on release to allow it to be shipped in parts and reassembled." Smyth says with the main spar underway, and with little time for detail drawings, the structural designers came to live at the build site until the wing was finished. "One of the biggest headaches," Smyth says, "was figuring out how to build and package the wing in such a way that we could fly it to Valencia and assemble it there. The most important decision we made was to build it so it all fitted back together like a Lego kit."

MORE PACE

In many ways the sailing season of 2009 was like the previous year, only more intense given that the wing was now under construction. The RC44 series got underway in April with a repeat win of the Cagliari Cup in Italy. Multihull racing was going on in X40s in between testing sessions of The Beast in San Diego. And a seemingly endless exchange of letters and legal motions and cross-motions continued between GGYC and SNG. In the end, it took a five-page, single-spaced document to list all that activity.

When summer commenced, the pace increased on all sides. The fact was, the Cup was only eight months away, and counting.

In July, mast 3 was stepped in *USA 17*, all 64.7 meters (212 feet, 3 inches) of it. Things on board got more interesting after that. The Beast started to fly. "We just started pushing the boat rather than stepping down early," Ross Halcrow says. "We were always triggering the alarms, but we were trying to make the boat go as fast as it could."

"The impressive thing," Dirk de Ridder says, "was we finally got to the limit of the foils. The curved foils were lifting the boat so far out of the water it was losing its grip. We were literally sailing on 50% of the float — there would be a meter of foil showing — that's how far the whole boat was lifting. It's a shame we never raced in those conditions, because that's when the boat is at its best.

"We might have hit 41 knots," de Ridder says, "but we were averaging 39. It's up there all the time. Speed is your friend in general on multihulls. With two hulls in the water, the boat feels uncomfortable. Once you fly a hull, the quicker you go the more comfortable it feels."

Added to the difficulty of trimming the mainsail with its 24-ton load — and trimming, when the boat is loaded up and approaching the edge, is critical — was the questionable ability of the soft sails to take the punishment. "Even if you are going 20 knots," Russell Coutts says, "with the apparent wind over the sails at 40 knots, the sails would eventually give up.

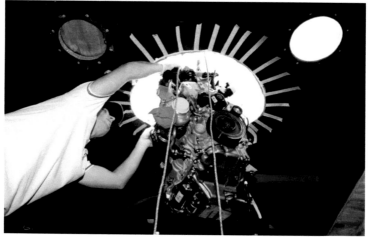

Having been allowed by the Supreme Court of New York in order to facilitate trimming the enormous loads the boat produced, an engine (BMW of course) is lowered aboard USA 17.

Structurally they couldn't handle it. They would flap and destroy themselves. If we had a 20-knot day, a wing would be much more reliable."

Chances of a 20-knot day were remote. Alinghi was looking for the lightest venue possible. But the idea of sails self-destructing from gale-force winds passing over them was a confounding new issue.

The trimming problem was solved on July 29, 2009, when the Supreme Court of New York ruled (among other things) to allow SNG's petition to use an engine on board the boats. "Nor does the court find that the change in the rules to permit movable ballast and power winches to trim sails in any way violates the controlling [Deed of Gift] rules," Justice Shirley Kornreich wrote. GGYC was dismayed about the decision, having fought hard against the engine not only as a breach of the international Racing Rules of Sailing, but as a dismissal of the Cup's 159-year tradition of using only manual (human) power to trim the sails. Power winches on an America's Cup yacht? The founders would be rolling over in their graves! On the other hand, if these outrageous racing machines were going to create such massive loads, an engine of 150 horsepower versus eight grinders developing two horsepower did make some sense.

Putting an engine on board created more work for the designers, who with the help of a cadre of BMW engineers had to figure out where best to put the thing, and for the builders who had to rip out the cockpit and rebuild it around the engine (twice). And it made eight of the hardest-working, most dedicated crewmembers — the grinders — redundant.

"The sailing team was really down on that decision," Jim Spithill says, "because the grinders had done all that lead-up work, and it was hard yards just getting the main up and down. They invested all those hours, then got pulled off the boat. I thought the team dealt with it, said okay, if that's the decision let's move on and make sure we do a good job of it. The good side was the engine made the boat incredibly rewarding to sail because you had all this horsepower on tap, meaning we could sail the boat like a dingy. With the grinders I had to drive a lot more, react to the wind. With the engine, we could trim more and steer less, which is the whole idea."

The law of unforeseen consequences kicked in. Now, with power to burn, it was the gear that started giving up. Dirk de Ridder said he would put brand-new traveler sheets on at the beginning of the day. At the end of the day he would throw them away because the winch drums got so hot they would literally melt the sheets. "The lines were lasting three weeks with human grinders," de Ridder says. "With the engine, and our ability to trim and ease constantly, the winch drums became sticking-hot. If you dumped water on them, and we did do that to cool them off, they would sizzle."

Legal Update – August 5, 2009

In a letter to GGYC, the United Arab Emirate of Ras Al-Khaimah is named by SNG as the venue for America's Cup XXXIII.

Legal Update – August 6, 2009

GGYC responds with a letter to SNG, stating objections to Ras Al-Khaimah as a venue, restating that Valencia is agreeable, and urging SNG to enter into discussions as to a mutually acceptable venue.

ALL THE MARBLES

No one at BMW Oracle Racing had ever heard of Ras Al-Khaimah (RAK), which is 100 miles northeast of Dubai on the Persian Gulf. RAK is part of the UAE, and is the closest emirate and trading partner with its neighbor just across the Strait of Hormuz: Iran. RAK was quickly evaluated as an extremely light-air venue, averaging wind velocities of three to five knots during the month of February.

In September, having not had a response to its letter from SNG, BMW Oracle Racing sent a crew out to have a look at RAK. "Our guys were well-received," Tom Ehman says. "But other than a hotel and a marina, there was nothing there. We would have had to build everything. And then the bad news: RAK is a large trading partner with Iran. Two Iranian-occupied islands are within a few miles of the racecourse specified by Alinghi. What if the police were to stop our containers? And if you had an Israeli stamp on your passport, they wouldn't let you in the country."

"I got a call from someone who had done some work there," Melinda Erkelens says, "and they said it was like the Wild West. They said not to drive around at night. Women must not take cabs by themselves. We started getting the information, and it was shockingly anti-Semitic. We couldn't believe Alinghi suggested it. By the end of September we knew we weren't comfortable going there."

Larry Ellison called Coutts and said we are not going to RAK. He ordered a full-out effort to discredit RAK as a proper venue. Tom Ehman, who with the team's general counsel Melinda Erkelens had helped steer the long and complicated court case from its inception in July, 2007, says two or three times during the campaign Russell Coutts got a few people together, leaned forward, put his hands on the table, and said, "This is for all the marbles!" Not going to RAK was one of those times.

Ellison made another key decision. He hired David Boies, a preeminent trial lawyer from the New York firm of Boies Schiller Flexner. Boies's high-profile cases include the defense of IBM in a 13-year antitrust suit brought by the Justice Department, and representation of the Justice Department against Microsoft. Boies's work has been the subject of two books. Boies would team up with Maureen Mahoney, an attorney from Latham & Watkins, LLP, New York, who had successfully handled the Challenger of Record appeal.

"Boies can prep in a matter of hours for a hearing that would take anyone else days," Melinda Erkelens says. "He has the ability to quickly memorize critical material and stand up and present it. When the judge got into an area he didn't understand, David was really good at bringing him back to what he knew, and moving things in the right direction. He is very impressive in court, and clearly well-respected by the court."

Boies filed a motion objecting to RAK as the site for America's Cup XXXIII. Among the arguments, supported by more than a dozen affidavits from notable people, was the assertion that RAK "presented grave safety concerns for the team members of an American challenger, named 'USA,' that flies an American flag on a 200-foot mast"; that it was inadvisable to hold a Cup race 50 nautical miles from Iranian territory and abutting water just 43 days after a UN deadline for the inspection of Iran's newly disclosed nuclear site; and it cited the risk of action against American participants and related watercraft by al-Qaeda cells. It was mentioned that the US Department of State had advised Americans traveling in RAK to maintain a low profile. "This is impossible," the motion read, "for an American racing team traveling with 200 people [competing in] a world-wide publicized America's Cup match in a vessel named USA the size of a baseball diamond . . ."

GGYC's motion to dismiss RAK as a venue was upheld by an order of the Supreme Court of New York on October 30, 2009. The court ordered the Cup venue back to Valencia. Tom Ehman says the defeat was huge, that Alinghi was shattered. SNG had been so convinced they would win the argument for RAK that Alinghi's catamaran had been lifted off

Lake Garda by helicopter and flown to Genoa, where it was put on a ship bound for RAK. By the time the decision was made, Alinghi had made camp in RAK and was sailing in the Persian Gulf.

When SNG lost, Alinghi had to pack up and ship everything back to Valencia. It was a logistical nightmare that cost them a full month. As a result, Alinghi and BMW Oracle Racing would arrive in Valencia at about the same time. BMW Oracle Racing might have won the venue battle, but getting there was equally rigorous for them.

BAD NEWS

On November 3, 2009, one week after the battle over RAK had been won by BMW Oracle Racing, the trimaran broke mast 3 while sailing off San Diego.

"We were flying," Dirk de Ridder says. "We had the mast moved forward that day, and we had moved the baby-stay up one notch. Mike Drummond was on board, and he said the mast didn't look right. We said okay, we'll bear away, we'll unload and put the baby-stay back where it was. I was sitting in the middle of the boat under the boom ready to ease the main because we were on full load, and the first four or five meters of ease is pretty loaded so you have to be watching the winch. We were literally five seconds from bearing away and there was this enormous crack, and the thing just came down."

'When it went," Jim Spithill says, "we were probably doing 20 knots going upwind, fully loaded. It was just a snap of the fingers, BANG! That's why it threw guys off the boat. The platform I was standing on split in half. I came down and hammered my ribs on the wheel. I saw our navigator, Mateo, standing looking at it and I screamed at him. He jumped out of the way. It was loud, the most violent thing I've ever been a part of. Rosco [trimmer Ross Halcrow] was the other concern because he was under it."

Halcrow was again wearing a helmet because the previous day he had noticed more bend in the boom and was afraid it might break. He was often working under it. "By the time I worked out the rig was coming down," Halcrow says, "all I had time to do was lie on the trampoline as close to the hull as possible. The boom ended up on top of me. The mast came to rest on my primary winch drum. It ended up about six inches above me where I was tucked into the netting next to the hull."

For Joey Newton, it was his worst fear realized. "I was terrified a lot of the time," Newton says. "All of us in the middle of the boat were on the firing line if something broke. We often talked about it. When the mast broke, I was trimming the traveler, looking up at the rig just as the mast popped to weather. I took two steps and jumped into the water. We were doing twenty knots. I remember hoping the chase boats wouldn't run over me. I stuck my head up and

---

Following pages: mast overboard, a sailors' nightmare.

the chase boats had stopped. I ended up 100 feet from the boat. I jumped pretty early. The guys give me grief about that. It was pretty terrifying when you think about it afterwards. At the time you act on instinct and get out of the road. Afterwards, lying in bed, you think whew, that was a bit scary.

"Rosco was under it, poor bloke. He needs to do more speed work so he can get out of the road quicker."

GOOD NEWS

The wingsail had arrived in San Diego on October 9. Core Builders had finished it in six months, ahead of schedule. It was a remarkable achievement given that it came at nearly the end of what had already been a two-and-a-half year, full-court press. When RAK was announced as the venue, Mike Drummond had immediately asked for an 8-meter (26-foot) extension on the wing to deal with the light wind there. The job took its toll. "It was deeply satisfying," Tim Smyth says. "Also impossible, but you're in a position where you can't back out. We replaced the team two times, burned people out, imported new people from all over the world. The reality is you work harder. We had one guy who worked 3,349 hours in one year. That's an average workweek of 67 hours. And every hour he worked he was productive. He's a legend around here."

In the end, Smyth and Turner put their backs firmly together against the plan to fly the wingsail to

Valencia. The idea was to ship the boat, finish work on the wing, and then fly it to Spain. Most of the wing was in manageable pieces, but the flaps were 7.5 meters (25 feet) square. Building protective boxes for the flaps was a big job. Getting those boxes into even the largest aircraft was going to be dicey. "We wrote a big report," Smyth says, "saying that flying the wing to Valencia was insanity. We said they had to take delivery of the wing in San Diego, test-sail it in San Diego, and ship it with the boat to Valencia. We had to pull six weeks out of the timeline for finishing the wing in order to do that. Part of that was time saved if we didn't have to screw around figuring out how to get it on a plane."

Getting it on a truck wasn't a whole lot easier. Well-padded cradles were built for the parts that would be rolling down the highway at 60 mph. "The wingsail was like a big, fragile egg," Tim Smyth says. "Any way we chose to rest it on itself was not ideal." When loaded, the truck was 30 millimeters (about 2 inches) under the maximum width allowed on US highways. The trip took five days. The flaps were trucked in flat-pack form. Seven builders from Core went to San Diego to assemble them in a 300-foot tent that was constructed in a parking lot. Thirty more builders spent four weeks in San Diego surfacing the wing parts with aircraft-grade film and joining them together.

The day mast 3 went down, the wingsail was less than a week from being finished. Mike Drummond was optimistic. He'd acquired a C-Class catamaran with a wingsail to get Spithill and others up to speed sailing with a wing. From that experience he knew the team wouldn't need a month of training to fine-tune the wing. Once the aerodynamic design was set, the wing would be set, as long as the mechanisms worked. "I thought if we had six weeks of sailing before the Cup, that would be enough," Drummond says. "And that turned out to be about what we had. Within a week of the first day we were sailing within 10 percent of our targeted performance. By match time we were over our targets much of the time."

First they had to get the wingsail on the boat. That process began at 4:30 a.m. the morning of November 10, 2009. Fifty people wheeled the enormous thing out of the tent and down the narrow passageway between the tent and the water. Without the 8-meter extension, it was 223 feet long, roughly 25 yards shorter than a football field.

Dave Hubbard originally formulated a system for raising and lowering the wing. Paul Bieker did the engineering detail design and execution. The system involved a crane to pick up the wing and maneuver it so its base could be attached to the mast step on the boat. A hoisting line was run from a fitting high on the wing to the end of a long strut (a "gin pole") and back to a primary winch on the boat. The strut pivoted on the mast step with a removable gimbaled bracket. A series of preventer lines were rigged to stabilize the wing. Eventually the crew got familiar enough with the system to be able to raise or lower the wing in an hour and a half. The first morning, it took about eight hours. After it was up, the many builders who

Longer then the wingspan of a Boeing 747, the massive wingsail was wheeled to the water in an early morning move by fifty people. Following pages: Raising and lowering the wingsail was an engineering feat. The first time the enormous wing was raised, the process took more than eight hours.

BY ROGER VAUGHAN • PAGE 127

had stayed to help with the raising of the wing quickly headed for the airport. Mast 4 had been ordered. "We had to build it," Tim Smyth says. "The whole campaign would be ruined if the wing wasn't any good."

WINGING IT

USA 17 left the dock under tow at around 2 p.m. that first day. It could have left earlier, but the crew and everyone else kept pausing to look up and gawk, like country bumpkins visiting Manhattan for the first time. Having a 200-foot mast towering above them had taken some getting used to. But looking up at a wing taller than the wingspan of a 747 perched on the slim main hull of a 115-foot multihull they were going to sail was unnerving.

"The most awe-inspiring part was when we stood it up that first morning," Ian Burns says. "It was so massive. It didn't look like it was meant to live on the ocean. It was like some piece of land-based architecture."

Gilles Martin-Raget photographed that memorable morning. "Most interesting about that moment when the wing went up," Martin-Raget says, "was that even if the designers and engineers were saying it should be okay, no one was sure because no one had ever done it before. The fact the boat went sailing that same day was totally amazing. It was the best day of the whole adventure, for me, emotionally, even stronger than the day we won the Cup."

After a minute or so under tow, *USA 17* was obviously sailing, so they cast off. The rig felt so right that it wasn't long before the crew was doing maneuvers in crowded San Diego Harbor, tacking and jibing, doing figure eights at 20 knots, things they wouldn't have dreamed of doing with the soft sail rig. "Sailing with the wing was . . . instantaneous!" Jim Spithill says. "It was like sailing a small boat. It was awesome, one of the best days we'd had."

Tom Ehman and Russell Coutts were in New York that day working in a conference room on the legal case. They watched over a San Diego webcam as the wingsail went up and the crew cast off and started sailing. Then Russell and Tom had to dash off to catch different planes at different airports. "Russell called me after hearing from Mike Drummond that they were doing figure eights in the harbor," Ehman said. "He was elated. I'd never heard him so excited."

Scott Ferguson was on board. "My heart was in my throat," he says. "It was emotional for me. We'd worked so hard to get the wing designed and built. To go from inside the tent where we had done a little testing, then through the lifting procedure, to going sailing, taking it slowly, making sure everything worked as we expected it to work, was surreal. As the day went on, we loaded it up more. Then Jimmy turned to me and said, Scotty, can we fly a hull? And I said well Jimmy, this is as good a time as any. It was quite a moment.

Following pages: Different angles capture the huge trimaran's blazing speed, and how the crew is dwarfed by the imposing vessel.

Coming in after that day I wasn't quite at the level of tears, but I felt pretty proud that something like that could go sailing, and fly a hull for the first time, which is a big moment when it comes to loading."

The trimmers had a learning curve for sailing with the wing. Today's trimmers keep an eye on the instruments, but they also look at sail shape. The wingsail didn't lend itself to that. The first day out everyone felt the boat was way below potential. De Ridder, Joey Newton, and Ross Halcrow met with Joseph Ozanne, and took his advice. "Joseph put a lot of time into the wing design and calculating the targets," de Ridder says. "So we started ignoring the feeling of whether it was right or wrong, and trimmed it to the targeted numbers. From then on we learned to trust the targets, and we were good."

Like anything innovative that's right out of the box, the wingsail would have its breaking-in period, with the emphasis on breaking. On November 13, one of the pins that secures an aft flap element and allows it to rotate jumped out of its socket, causing damage. Brad Webb went aloft and popped it back into place. Note to design and build teams: longer pins needed. On November 16, the bottom of the lowest flap broke off where the traveler attached. The flap would need to be rebuilt and reinforced. These were incidentals. Nothing serious malfunctioned.

But there were some serious off-the-boat han-dling problems that put the wing in jeopardy, and, as Tim Smyth said, put his stomach in his throat more than once. As predicted, wing logistics were a nightmare. On December 9, the wing was lowered and disassembled for shipping. The flaps were packed in huge, special boxes that measured 7.5 by 7.5 meters (25 by 25 feet). The boxes had soft tops because they would be stored below deck on the ship. An unusually massive rainstorm for San Diego dumped a load of water on each of the boxes that had been left outside, uncovered. The soft tops caved in on the contents, breaking frames and ruining the film covering on all but two of the eleven flaps. One plan was to return the flaps to Anacortes for repair, then fly them to Valencia so they would arrive at the same time as the ship and afford more sailing time. Smyth and Turner convinced the sailing team to ship them with the boat while they built replacement parts in Anacortes. They would repair the flaps in Spain.

Three days later, while loading the main element onto the ship, the wing caught a breeze and tried to fly. A strop broke, the main element dropped, frames were broken. It was an accident that could have spelled the end of the campaign. One couldn't help wondering where Larry Ellison was when he heard the news. "They didn't tell me," Ellison says with a chuckle. "At least not until it had been successfully repaired a few days later.

"The wing can take a lot," Ellison says. "One horrible night in Valencia it gusted to 59 knots. We had several boats out trying to keep the trimaran into

Following pages: During a tack, Jim Spithill hustles the 60-feet from wheel to wheel as the crew tacks the jib and trims the wing.

the wind. But when you have a 23-story wing, there's no such thing as heading into the wind. Wind speeds are different at different heights along the wing, and that moves the apparent wind angle. If you think you can stop the tri by heading into the wind, I don't think so. You're thinking of the sailing you did the first fifty years of your life. This is different."

"We couldn't fix the wing before it shipped," Tim Smyth says. "It was shrink wrapped, and that process had taken two days. We just added those repairs to the list. We got a Core Builders Invasion Force ready to embark for Spain. We were thirty-two guys and a huge air-freight box that measured 8 by 2 by 2 meters full of tools and parts. We stopped work on mast number 4 – a replacement for the shattered mast number 3 — because we were out of resources. We had to build flap parts, and we needed people in Spain to work on the wing. It was like a military campaign at this point, responding to crises. Lisa Watson, our team travel coordinator, was heroic, somehow getting us all over there during the Christmas holiday, and finding us accommodations."

PERILS OF VALENCIA

The ship arrived at Valencia on January 4, 2010, five weeks before the America's Cup match. By the time boat and gear were unpacked and reassembled, and the flaps and main wing element had been repaired, the first sailing day was January 19. Having evaluated the wing's performance in San Diego, Mike Drummond had the shore team affix the extra 7.4-meter element he had ordered for RAK. Scott Ferguson admits his attention was riveted on the new piece that first day on the water in Valencia. "If it had let go, it wouldn't have just flown away," he says. "It had a control line through it, so it could have swung down and caused damage." The extra piece stayed in place.

What malfunctioned that day was a halyard lock. The furled headsail had a massive swivel on the head. When the lock let go, the rolled-up sail fell to the deck, with the swivel taking out two control arms on the wing on the way down. A shuttle line was subsequently rigged forward to keep the head of the sail away from the mast on the way up and down. One more job for bowman Brad Webb.

The next day, coal dust from a nearby plant jammed the mechanism controlling one of the dagger foils, costing the team a half day of sailing. The wingsail was being lowered every night for minor repairs, which was time-consuming. The clock was ticking inexorably toward the first scheduled race on February 8.

On January 23, the sailing team stayed out when the wind freshened to 25 knots. It was an amazing, high-speed sail, a true confidence-builder for the sailors. They noticed *Alinghi* coming out, then quickly turning around without raising sails and heading back in. "It was a classic moment," Brad Webb says. "They elected not to sail in conditions that we were loving. That cranked us up."

Before they knew it they'd sailed ten miles up-wind under freshening conditions into the biggest chop they'd ever been in. It was very wet on board. Then they bore off and started rocketing downwind at 35 knots, hitting 40 more than once, with water flying everywhere. The only downside was that the boat hadn't been waterproofed for heavy conditions. Suddenly the engine stopped. Everything else stopped as well, because the PLCs (programmable logic controllers) got soaked and stopped working. The PLCs control everything on board, winches, engine revs, hydraulics — they even tell the winches when to change gears. The entire boat was dead.

It was a difficult sail home. Even the winch pedestals had been removed when the engine came on board. They used some minimal backup systems they had in place. "Joey Allen, our coach, said come on guys, let's just fix this thing," Brad Webb recalls. "A veteran ocean sailor, Joey was thinking duct tape, a Leatherman, and some wire. We explained to Joey that the entire boat is electrical. The electronics team was pretty pissed. It took them two and a half days to rebuild everything. We didn't do that again."

That evening, while they were removing the wing from the boat, one of the lifting lines broke. The trailing edge of the wing dropped and smacked into the dock, causing considerable damage. If the leading edge had hit the dock, the campaign would have been over. As it was, repairs took several days.

The frustrating litany of damage continued. On January 28, a control arm on the wing broke while sailing. It was thought to be the result of damage sustained when the wing was dropped. On February 4, just four days before the scheduled Race 1, a frame in the 4th flap broke while sailing, offering Mike Drummond the opportunity to make a decision that many say permanently changed BMW Oracle Racing's momentum for the good. While sailing, the crew had heard a strange noise, but kept sailing. When they came in, they discovered what it was and had a discussion. Instead of lowering the wing and taking a day out of sailing to give it a proper fix in the shop, Drummond ordered a quick fix. He sent Andrew Walker from the shore team up the rig with a kit of carbon-fiber panels, glue, and a rivet gun. Walker stuck the damaged piece back together.

"I did it partly to get the team out of training mentality and into racing mentality," Drummond says. "In racing, things aren't always perfect. You have to make do. No reason we couldn't fix it and keep sailing. If we failed to fix it, it wouldn't be catastrophic. The upside was another day of sailing. It sparked more urgency within the team about the impending racing. I think they went out and did a bunch of jibes for the first time." The quick fix got the team two days on the water before another bad weather window came through. During that time, the wing was lowered and properly fixed.

The drama wasn't over. A couple days later a storm blew through the Valencia waterfront. "It blew 60 to 70 knots," Mark Turner says. "It was fresh. It was precarious, a very uncomfortable twelve hours. It blew the sides off the tent covering the wing. Alinghi's sail loft was leveled. I'm standing next to the wingsail thinking this thing is over, this tent is coming down. It would have destroyed the wing." But after a team-inclusive, all-hands-on-deck call to reinforce it, the tent held. From then on, The Beast and its giant wing started behaving much better.

RACE 1

Look at the videotape of Race 1 from 4:45 to the start and what makes you keep replaying that segment is the speed *USA 17* carries into the starting box. The boat is flying on one float, a big black predator coming in for the kill at full speed, which happened to be over 20 knots. The backlighting of the shot adds a surrealistic, computer-generated element. But no, it's for real, and it's stunning.

It was clear that *Alinghi*, with Ernesto Bertarelli at the helm, was caught unawares. *Alinghi*, the burdened vessel on port tack, was slow, sailing with both hulls in the water. Instead of jibing away and buying some time, *Alinghi* sailed right into *USA 17*'s path. The image of *USA 17* with its white bows and black hulls as a screaming eagle diving in with claws extended is irresistible. Penalty to *Alinghi*, meaning they would have to do a 360-degree turn before finishing. In a multihull, a 360-degree turn takes forever.

"We had talked about going after him prior to the start," tactician John Kostecki says. "The dialup [where the starboard tack boat pins the opponent head to wind] is a very powerful move. Jimmy thought we'd have a shot. For sure it's the right thing to do as long as you can handle your boat properly."

"To have a chance," Jim Spithill says, "I knew we had to be red lining. So we came in lit up. And it worked. We got the penalty." But then Spithill got greedy, carried on and went head to wind with *Alinghi*. At that moment he might have been thinking about his friend and coach Philippe Presti, who cautioned him against the dialup. Presti has been working with Spithill since they were both with the Prada team for the 2007 America's Cup. Presti was Prada's trial-horse skipper. Presti knew there had been precious little time to practice downspeed maneuvering. He had told Spithill he was worried *USA 17* could get stuck in irons. "As it turned out," Spithill says with a grin, "Philippe was bang on.

"It just highlighted how under-prepared both boats were," Spithill says, "them getting the penalty, and us getting stuck in irons. There was an opportunity with 1:40 to go where we could have just sailed away, gone off and been ahead with their penalty turn in our pocket. But we were all so focused on the other boat we lost track of time . . ." It was the only time Spithill missed that large rudder on the main hull that he had so happily removed.

With both boats well above the start line, *USA 17* was stuck in irons. It didn't help that a winch suffered a temporary lapse, causing a delay in unrolling the jib. No one on *USA 17* ever mentioned the problem with the winch. "It's part of the culture of this team," Larry Ellison says. "There are no excuses. If we lost, we made a mistake or didn't sail well." Meanwhile *Alinghi* was able to bear away, round the pin, and start just fifteen seconds late. It seemed to take an age for *USA 17* to get into motion, return to the line, and start 90 seconds behind *Alinghi*. "The best thing," Jim Spithill says, "is it didn't faze the guys. When we sailed back into it, it gave them a massive boost."

The first five or ten minutes of the first upwind leg of any America's Cup is always thoroughly riveting for sailors and onlookers alike. After years of designing, building, sailing, logistics, public relations, legal actions, and scuttlebutt, it's the first time the competitors have lined up for real. Finally, the only important question — which boat is faster? — is answered. America's Cup XXXIII was no exception. *Alinghi* was 660 meters ahead when *USA 17* finally crossed the start line. After three minutes, *Alinghi* was 435 meters ahead. And while *USA 17* had started further to leeward on the line, the black boat was now to windward of *Alinghi*'s track, and increasing weather gauge all the time, looking rock-solid sailing on one float. *Alinghi* was often having trouble flying a hull.

After getting stuck in irons, USA 17 *trails* Alinghi. *Sailing higher and faster, it didn't take* USA 17 *long to pass the Swiss boat. Following pages: Spithill at his steering station, 50 feet above the water; the 115-foot by 90-foot multihull flying on one, thin float.*

Tom Ehman was BMW Oracle Racing's representative on the race-committee boat, alongside representatives from SNG. Ehman says five minutes in, the SNG guys were looking dismayed. "I said to Harold Bennett, the principle race officer, loud enough so the SNG guys could hear, 'Think we're sailing in different wind?' Harold answered back loud and clear, 'No way, you're higher and faster.'"

"Within ten seconds of Jimmy getting the boat going," Larry Ellison says, "I said we're heading in a different direction than they are. You could see that immediately. A minute later we were closing on them. We were a lot higher, a lot faster. At least 2 knots faster, 4 degrees higher. And this is their ideal condition? They are screwed. It was stunning."

Alinghi started with the wrong headsail. It was too big. But they changed heads'ls five minutes up the 20-mile leg. Sailmaker Craig Phillips says *Alinghi*'s mainsail was also too big, causing a lot of drag. "They had way too much rag up," Phillips says. Ten or fifteen minutes up the course, *USA 17* hit its 15-knot wind-speed crossover where the wingsail was more effective without a headsail, and furled its jib. At that point the boat seemed to sail even higher, even faster. The upwind sailing angle for *USA 17* was around 7 degrees, believe it or not. Those used to watching monohulls of the sort used in America's Cup XXXII, with upwind sailing angles of around 30 degrees, were scratching their heads in disbelief. *USA 17*'s downwind sailing angle was 25 degrees. It's all about boat speed bringing the apparent wind forward. Aside from a down-speed period for *USA 17* of about 10 minutes, probably caused by a right-hand shift, during which their lead was cut to 150 meters, the black boat just kept stretching out. With multihulls, large gains and losses are normal because the boats accelerate so quickly in puffs. In a match race, the two boats will often find themselves sailing in different wind conditions, which can reverse fortunes. But at the weather mark, *USA 17* had a lead of 3:24.

Downwind had always been the worry. The catamaran is considerably lighter. It was long assumed the cat would be faster downwind. But *USA 17* carried on, stretching its lead on the second and final leg to 15:25 at the finish. "I kept looking over my shoulder," Spithill says, "and watching them getting smaller. That was the biggest surprise for me."

Larry Ellison got on board after the finish and drove the boat home. "We were going fast because there was more wind," Ellison says. "I was really enjoying it. Russell came up to me and said, Larry, you're not driving during the race, so you cannot win us the America's Cup. You can, however, lose us the America's Cup BY FLIPPING THIS THING — BACK OFF, WE'RE NOT RACING!!"

Did Ellison consider driving during the America's Cup? "Sure, I thought about it," he says. "I had practiced. I thought I could have done it pretty safely, and it was all about safety because we were so much faster. We initially thought the crossover where they would be faster was 7 to 8 knots of wind.

Flanked by Jim Spithill (left) and Russell Coutts, BMW Oracle Racing skipper Larry Ellison addresses the media after Race 1.

But I'm not sure there was a crossover anywhere. I don't think they could have beaten us in 4 knots. And if we ever had conditions favorable to us — 20 knots — we could have finished before they got to the weather mark.

"But the fact is, Jimmy put in all the work, all the training, all the time. Was he the right guy to drive the boat? You bet. He was our best guy. I figured if Russell could get off the wheel, then I sure as hell could."

RACE 2

After waiting more than six hours for wind on February 14, 2010, Race 2 of America's Cup XXXIII got underway in a most disappointing fashion. *Alinghi*, with the starboard entry this day, committed an unfathomable error when it prematurely sailed into the box, the top of which is defined by the starting line. In a match race, the two boats must not enter the box until the five-minute signal. It's elementary, like obeying a caution flag in motor sports, or obeying the speed limit on pit lane. Once again, *Alinghi* was penalized before the start, but this time for an unforced mental error. By the time *Alinghi* jibed around the race committee boat and re-entered the box, she was over a minute late. *USA 17* had entered at 4:40, and was out of reach of the starboard-tack boat. *USA 17* harassed *Alinghi* from behind on the way to the starting line, got a fast start on starboard tack at the pin end, and sped out to the left side, leaving *Alinghi* executing a painfully slow tack and crossing the line a full minute late.

Alinghi went to the right. *USA 17* could have covered, but chose not to. Conditions were very shifty, with wind speed fluctuating. The Swiss picked up more breeze on the right, and sailed into a header. They tacked, and came out strong on starboard tack, making a huge gain. *USA 17* tacked to leeward and ahead of *Alinghi*. The Virtual Eye graphic system that enhances the telecast of Cup racing uses computers and GPS signals from both boats to calculate an ahead/behind line relative to the next mark. Virtual Eye had *USA 17* behind at that point, but they would be first to the layline. *Alinghi* looked to be performing much better upwind than in Race 1. The two boats seemed about even in speed. There was a change of helmsman on *Alinghi*. On the Swiss boat's first tack, accomplished multihull ocean racer Loïck Peyron was seen replacing Ernesto Bertarelli at the wheel. *Alinghi* sailors said after the race they had their boat cranked full on, with load sensor alarms ringing constantly. They had no choice. Lose Race 2 and they would lose the Cup.

USA 17 tactician John Kostecki had a plan. As *USA 17* hit the layline to the first mark, Kostecki waited five more boat lengths before he called the tack. With only a two-boat-length lead, *Alinghi* couldn't tack under *USA 17* without either tacking too close and committing a foul or possibly missing the layline. If the two boats had been monohulls, a well-executed tack under *USA 17*'s lee bow by *Alinghi* would have been the proper move. But multihulls don't carry enough momentum to employ that tactic. *Alinghi* kept on. *USA 17* (now on port tack) dipped *Alinghi*. The Swiss boat tacked ever so slowly after a boat length. Now *USA 17* had the inside position at the mark, and, suddenly, the lead.

"My experience with *Groupama* and the X40s showed me that, given the starboard mark rounding,

Following pages: In Race 2, the two boats seemed more even in speed. USA 17 **sailed upwind just 7 degrees off the wind, and downwind it was faster than** Alinghi, **steady as a rock.**

port tack is stronger into the mark than starboard," John Kostecki explains. "The starboard tacker has to maneuver, and maneuvers in a multihull are slow. It's a standard move, not much of a big deal." Despite Kostecki's modesty, veteran observers said it was the key tactical call of the Cup match.

No more big calls were necessary. *USA 17* led by :28 at the first mark of the three-legged course. The lead was 2:44 at Mark 2. While *Alinghi* struggled down the third leg trying to keep a hull flying, *USA 17* looked like it was on rails, steady as a rock heeled up on one float, stretching its lead constantly. Spithill's wheel motion was minimal. The cameras showed that the trimaran's center hull was bone dry. With *Alinghi*'s penalty turn, the finishing delta was 5:26.

As *USA 17* crossed the finish line, TV New Zealand's commentator Peter Montgomery pronounced, "The America's Cup is, once again, America's cup!"

The sailors were ecstatic. The celebration was raucous and well-deserved. But as the champagne flowed and the ceremonial dockside dunkings and hoisting of the America's Cup began, there wasn't a person on the dock who didn't consider, for a moment, this fact: prior to the race on February 10, 2010, *USA 17* had never sailed around the America's Cup course without stopping to fix something. In the last three days, when it counted, they had twice sailed the course uninterrupted. Timing really is everything. The heroic effort behind this extraordinary mission that many thought might be impossible, right up to the last week, came together at just the right time.

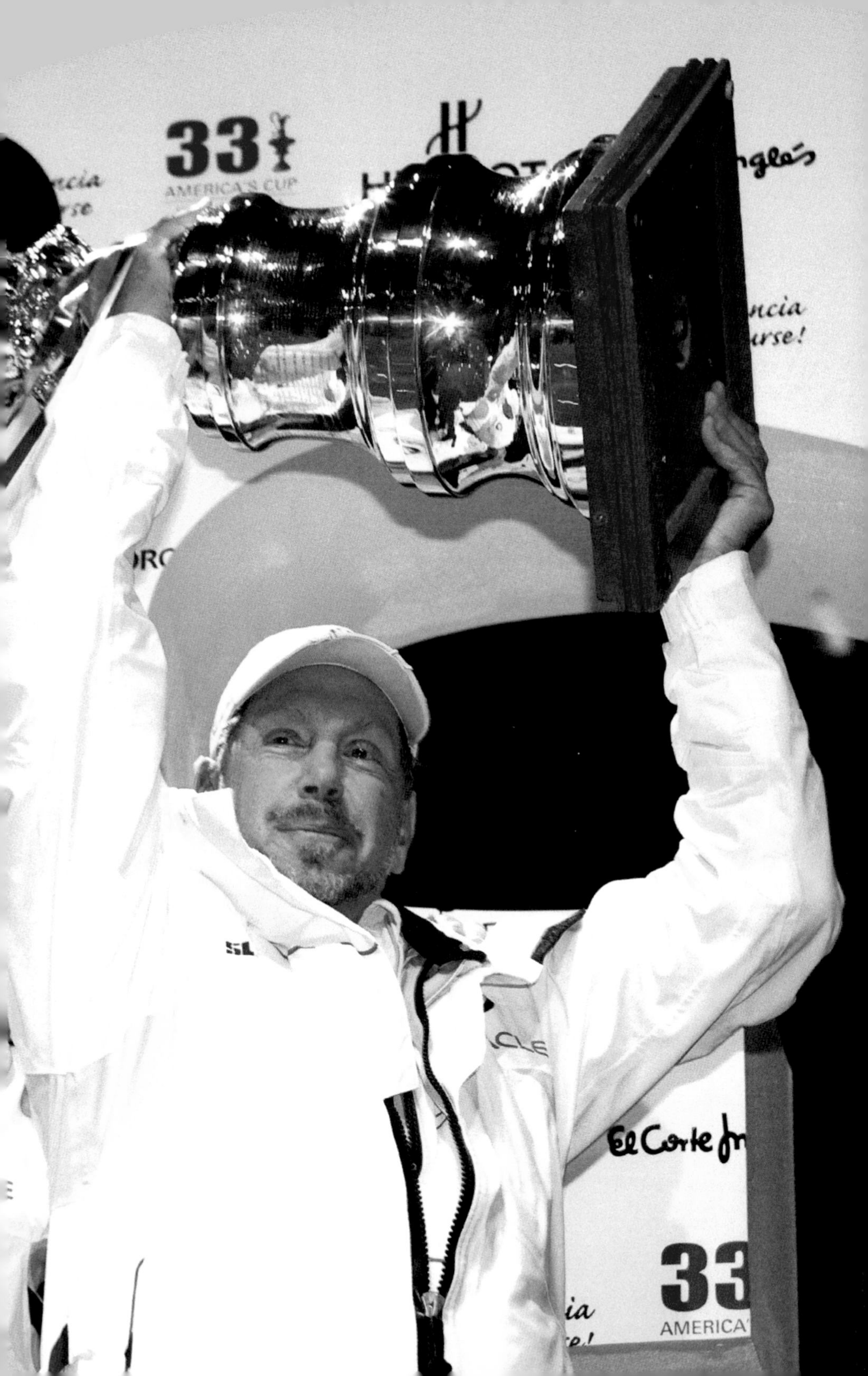
33
AMERICA'S CUP

LAST WORDS

Russell Coutts says that the complexity of this Cup made it the most satisfying of his four wins from a leadership point of view. He says it was tough not be to sailing, to be land-bound two Cups in a row. "I made an early decision not to sail," Coutts says. "Then it got entangled from a legal and technical standpoint, and when it went to a multihull I knew I didn't have time to train and get myself up to a level where I could sail."

Was beating Ernesto Bertarelli particularly sweet? Coutts smiles. "Yeah," he says quietly, "yes, it was."

Jim Spithill says he got thoroughly addicted to sailing The Beast. "At the end of a day of training I'd say oh no, is the sun really going down? We have to stop? I couldn't wait to get back on it the next day." When the campaign was over, Spithill found himself in a state of depression for a couple months. He solved that by getting into A- and C-Class multihull competitions. Those boats would provide enough adrenaline for him.

Brad Webb was relieved when it was over. "I wanted the day of the Cup to arrive. I wanted to go race, win, and get it done. That's what kept me going.

Preceeding pages: Spithill and Coutts are all smiles as Ellison hoists the America's Cup. Representing the Golden Gate Yacht Club in San Francisco, Ellison's BMW Oracle racing campaign successfully brought the cup back home.

Nothing really bad happened, even with the mast going down, but we thought about it all the time. Our coach Joey Allen was a godsend. One day he said to us, take the time to look around you, because you are doing something that will never be done again, and you guys are lucky. I used to do that, take five seconds here and there and say yeah, this is really cool, before returning to the reality of how hard it was. I relish the win, the success, but I don't miss it."

Mike Drummond says the budget was sufficient, even generous, but in the end, every America's Cup campaign runs out of time. "No amount of budget can buy more time," Drummond says.

Mark Turner: "It's taken me personally four months to unwind from the event. It was the pressure. I've never felt anything like it in my life. Pressure was the constant theme for more than two years to make it happen. In the end you wonder how you got through the sheer magnitude of work, and the time frame to do it in. But I'll say one thing. We simply out-built the other team."

Larry Ellison, who sailed aboard *USA 17* in the last race, raised the trophy he decided to go after ten years ago as champagne rained down upon him and the crowd roared. Then he said into the microphone, "This is amazing, awesome, better than that."

Made in the USA
Monee, IL
15 June 2021